GENESIS 25–33

Jacob's

Blessing

A Guided Discovery for Groups and Individuals

Kevin and Louise Perrotta

LOYOLA PRESS.
A JESUIT MINISTRY

Chicago

LOYOLA PRESS.
A JESUIT MINISTRY

3441 N. Ashland Avenue
Chicago, Illinois 60657
(800) 621-1008
www.loyolapress.com

Nihil Obstat
Reverend John G. Lodge, S.S.L., S.T.D.
Censor Deputatus
May 10, 2003

Imprimatur
Most Reverend Raymond E. Goedert, M.A., S.T.L., J.C.L.
Vicar General
Archdiocese of Chicago
May 12, 2003

The *Nihil Obstat* and *Imprimatur* are official declarations that a book is free of doctrinal and moral error. No implication is contained therein that those who have granted the *Nihil Obstat* and *Imprimatur* agree with the content, opinions, or statements expressed. Nor do they assume any legal responsibility associated with publication.

The Scripture quotations contained herein are from the New Revised Standard Version Bible: Catholic Edition, copyright © 1993 and 1989 by the Division of Christian Education of the National Council of the Churches of Christ in the U.S.A. Used by permission. All rights reserved. Subheadings in Scripture quotations have been added by Kevin and Louise Perrotta.

To C. M. C.

The full text of Pope John Paul II's prayer for families (p. 18) can be found at the end of his apostolic exhortation *The Role of the Christian Family in the Modern World,* which can be viewed at www.vatican.va/holy_father/john_paul_ii/apost_exhortations/documents/hf_jp-ii_exh_19811122_familiaris_consortio_en.html.

The excerpt about John-Paul Floyd (p. 83) is from Gregory Floyd, *A Grief Unveiled* (Brewster, Mass.: Paraclete Press, 1999), 109–10, 112, 154. Used with permission of the publisher.

Editor's note: Kevin and Louise worked together on this booklet. Kevin wrote the introduction; the material in weeks 1, 2, and 6; and the essays on pages 20, 34, and 84. Louise wrote the material in weeks 3, 4, and 5 and the essays on pages 58, 72, and 88.

Interior design by Kay Hartmann/Communique Design
Illustration by Charise Mericle Harper

ISBN-13: 978-0-8294-1542-1
ISBN-10: 0-8294-1542-4

Printed in the United States of America
17 18 19 20 20 22 23 Bang 10 9 8 7 6 5 4 3 2

Contents

How to Use This Guide

You might compare the Bible to a national park. The park is so large that you could spend months, even years, getting to know it. But a brief visit, if carefully planned, can be enjoyable and worthwhile. In a few hours you can drive through the park and pull over at a handful of sites. At each stop you can get out of the car, take a short trail through the woods, listen to the wind blowing through the trees, get a feel for the place.

In this booklet, we will read the main portion of the story of Jacob: Genesis 25–33. We will take a leisurely walk through the six readings, giving ourselves the opportunity to think carefully about what we are reading and what it means for our lives today. Jacob's life certainly makes for interesting reading, but it also gives us a great deal to reflect on.

This guide provides everything you need to explore the story of Jacob in six discussions—or to do a six-part exploration on your own. The introduction on page 6 will prepare you to get the most out of your reading. The weekly sections provide background and explanations that will help you grasp what this biblical narrative means for you today. Equally important, each section supplies questions that will launch your group into fruitful discussion, helping you to both investigate the biblical text for yourself and learn from one another. If you're using the booklet by yourself, the questions will spur your personal reflection.

Each discussion is meant to be a *guided discovery*.

Guided. None of us is equipped to read the Bible without help. We read the Bible *for* ourselves but not *by* ourselves. Scripture was written to be understood and applied in the community of faith. So each week "A Guide to the Reading," drawing on the work of both modern biblical scholars and Christian writers of the past, supplies background and explanations. The guide will help you grasp the message of Genesis. Think of it as a friendly park ranger who points out noteworthy details and explains what you're looking at so you can appreciate things for yourself.

Discovery. The purpose is for *you* to interact with this biblical story. "Questions for Careful Reading" is a tool to help you dig into the text and examine it carefully. "Questions for Application" will help you consider what these words mean for your life here and now. Each week concludes with an "Approach to Prayer" section that helps you respond to God's word. Supplementary "Living Tradition" and "Saints in the Making" sections offer the thoughts and experiences of Christians past and present. By showing what the story of Jacob and its themes have meant to others, these sections will help you consider what they mean for you. "Between Discussions" sections offer further background and points for reflection.

How long are the discussion sessions? We've assumed you will have about an hour and a half when you get together. If you have less time, you'll find that most of the elements can be shortened somewhat.

Is homework necessary? You will get the most out of your discussions if you read the weekly material and prepare answers to the questions in advance of each meeting. If participants are not able to prepare, have someone read the "Guide to the Reading" sections aloud at the points where they appear.

What about leadership? If you happen to have a world-class biblical scholar in your group, by all means ask him or her to lead the discussions. In the absence of any professional Scripture scholars, or even accomplished amateur biblical scholars, you can still have a first-class Bible discussion. Choose two or three people to take turns as facilitators, and have everyone read "Suggestions for Bible Discussion Groups" (page 92) before beginning.

Does everyone need a guide? a Bible? Everyone in the group will need his or her own copy of this guide. It contains the entire text of the readings from Genesis, so a Bible is not absolutely necessary—but each participant will find it useful to have one. You should have at least one Bible on hand for your discussions. (See page 96 for recommendations.)

How do we get started? Before you begin, take a look at the suggestions for Bible discussion groups (page 92) or individuals (page 95).

Jacob and Family

A pious but somewhat passive father. A decisive but unscrupulous mother. Twin boys, opposites in temperament, each favored by one parent. Envy, disrespect, deception, rage. It sounds like the checklist of a family headed toward counseling. But this is a family selected by God to play a crucial role in his saving plan for the world—the family of Isaac and Rebekah and their sons, Esau and Jacob. They are the ancestors of the people of Israel. Jacob, in fact, is the man after whom Israel is named (he receives the name Israel in the course of the story we are about to read).

The account of Isaac and Rebekah's relationally challenged family illustrates one of the Bible's most remarkable features: its frank display of heroes' sins. The Old Testament historians narrate in damning detail how King David, the golden boy of Israel's golden age, committed adultery with the wife of one of his military officers and then used the man's courage in battle to bring about his death. The Gospel writers tell us that as soon as Jesus was arrested, Peter, the disciple on whom he had lavished the greatest privileges, swore up and down that he did not even know Jesus. In the story we will be reading, Jacob exploits his elderly father's physical disability to deprive his brother of his inheritance.

The Bible can be honest about its heroes' failings because it is less concerned with honoring them than with honoring God. God is the true hero of the biblical story. When human beings reject his path of integrity and faithfulness, God takes the opportunity to offer forgiveness and open a road to restoration. Nothing more sharply highlights this divine mercy than God's dealings with Jacob.

The Bible's honesty about the failings of Jacob and his kin—and its emphasis on God's grace—makes this story accessible to all of us. We all have firsthand knowledge of envy. Most of us have told our share of lies. Certainly we all need God's mercy. Thus we can all find points of connection with the story of Jacob. At every turn, it sparks reflections about our own experience of sin, repentance, and grace. The account of Jacob is like a great movie, novel, or play—it gives us much to ponder with regard to our own lives.

Jacob's story is part of a larger one. Most immediately, it is part of a family saga. The saga, in turn, is part of the story of the people of Israel and the Church.

The Bible traces the unfolding of God's purposes for humanity. In an early phase of this plan—after creation and after humankind's refusal to cooperate with God (Genesis 1–11)—God selects a couple named Abraham and Sarah, originally residents of what is now southern Iraq, and makes them participants in his plan. After guiding them on a long journey that ends in present-day Israel and Palestinian territories, God promises to give their descendants the land and to make them into a nation through whom the peoples of the world will be blessed (12:1–7; throughout this guide, chapter and verse numbers refer to the book of Genesis unless otherwise noted). God renews this promise to Isaac, Abraham and Sarah's son, and, as we shall see, to Isaac's son Jacob. Jacob's twelve sons become the ancestors of twelve tribes—groups of shepherding people—with whom God makes a covenant through a leader named Moses. The people formed by this covenant are called Israel. The Israelites go through many ups and downs in their relationship with God over a period of centuries. Ultimately, God himself is born as a member of this people, taking on our human nature in the person of Jesus of Nazareth.

On its own, the story of Jacob is a tale of God's unpredictable kindness: a young man goes wrong, but God nevertheless protects him and leads him to a better life. In the context of the larger biblical history, Jacob's story is a striking instance of God's tendency to select unlikely people to be key players in his saving plan for the world. The story of Jacob thus reflects God's amazing grace and God's amazing choosing.

To read the story of Jacob in light of all its connections with the larger story of salvation would be a daunting task. Since this guide is meant to be introductory, we will focus simply on the story itself—in fact, only chapters 25 through 33 (Jacob's story continues through chapter 50). Once you have become familiar with the account of Jacob in these chapters, you will be in a better position to explore its connections with the rest of the Bible.

The story of Jacob is artfully told. The authors were master storytellers who gave attention to the smallest details. Theirs is artistry in miniature. In an average translation, the story we are about to read covers only a dozen pages. Within this short narrative, phrases, single words, even silences carry a weight of meaning.

If you match the authors' careful writing with careful reading, you will not regret the effort. Close reading of the story will provoke questions. Once you are looking for answers, you will be more alert to details that you might otherwise have ignored. The process of lingering over details, asking questions, and searching for answers will lead you into the heart of the story.

For example, consider Jacob's statement to Isaac in 27:20. Jacob speaks to his father of "the Lord your God." The careful reader will pause and wonder, "Why does Jacob say *your* God? Isn't Isaac's God also Jacob's God? What kind of relationship does Jacob have with God? How is Jacob's relationship with God reflected in—and affected by—his relationship with his father, Isaac?" Having asked these questions, we will be more likely to notice clues that the authors have provided to the answers. Thus we will pay attention when Jacob later describes his family and possessions as "graciously given" by God (33:5). Jacob no longer speaks of God as someone else's deity. The simple absence of the adjective *your* betokens a change in Jacob's relationship with the Creator—a change that lies at the center of the entire story.

In this guide, the Questions for Careful Reading and the Guides to the Reading each week will point out such details and raise such questions. Of course, it will then be up to you to ponder the questions—and to reflect on the issues that the story raises for your life and for the world today.

We have referred to the "authors." Who were they? The story of Jacob, like the other accounts of his family—from his grandparents Abraham and Sarah to his grandchildren—was handed on in oral traditions, possibly for centuries, among the ancient Israelites. The stories were probably written down and edited by many scribes over a long period, perhaps from the tenth to the fifth centuries before Christ. The writers may have woven together varying traditions, which may explain some of the occasional rough edges and unevenness (we will meet an example of this in week 6, in the story of Jacob's mysterious wrestling match). Nevertheless, the final product is a masterful series of family tales that convey much about God's purposes in history and his ways of relating to human beings.

In brief, the authorship of the Jacob stories is a complex subject. For our purposes in this guide, however, it is enough to know that the authors were sages of ancient Israel inspired by the Holy Spirit.

A word about geography: as our story begins, Isaac and Rebekah are living at an oasis in the Sinai desert called Beer-lahai-roi. Later, they move north to the edge of the settled land at Beersheba (in the south of the modern state of Israel). From there, Jacob travels north, stopping in Bethel, in what is now the Palestinian territory often referred to as the West Bank, and continues on through present-day Syria. His journey takes him to Haran, today in south-central Turkey. On his return, Jacob journeys back through Syria into present-day Jordan, where the climactic scene in chapter 33 occurs. Later Jacob goes to Shechem (today in the West Bank). Esau's residence in Seir is in the south of modern Jordan.

The immediate background to the opening events of the story is as follows. Some years earlier, Abraham sends a servant from Beersheba to Haran to find a bride for his son Isaac from among Abraham's relatives. At a well near Haran, the servant meets Rebekah, one of Abraham's nieces. Seeing God's hand in this chance encounter, he suggests that Rebekah become Isaac's wife. Her family assents to the marriage (significantly for our present story, her brother, Laban, seems to be won over by the signs of Abraham's wealth). Asked by her family if she would like to put off her journey to her new home while the family celebrates, Rebekah answers instead, "Let's go!" The servant escorts her to Beersheba, where she and Isaac are wed.

CONFLICT BEGINS AT CONCEPTION

Questions to Begin

15 minutes
Use a question or two to get warmed up for the reading.

---

1 What kind of baby were you?
- ❏ I was a "good" baby. (I slept a lot and didn't cry much.)
- ❏ I was generally cheerful and easygoing.
- ❏ I was fairly demanding.
- ❏ My birth signaled the beginning of a period of severe sleep-deprivation for my mother.
- ❏ I was a real stinker.

---

2 How early in life do children's distinctive personalities begin to appear?

---

3 Describe a situation in which you made a quick decision. How happy were you with the results?

5 minutes
Read the passage aloud. Let individuals take turns reading paragraphs.

The Reading: Genesis 25:20–34; 26:34–27:17

A Difficult Pregnancy

25:20 Isaac was forty years old when he married Rebekah, daughter of Bethuel the Aramean of Paddan-aram, sister of Laban the Aramean. 21 Isaac prayed to the LORD for his wife, because she was barren; and the LORD granted his prayer, and his wife Rebekah conceived. 22 The children struggled together within her; and she said, "If it is to be this way, why do I live?" So she went to inquire of the LORD. 23 And the LORD said to her,

> "Two nations are in your womb,
>   and two peoples born of you shall be divided;
> the one shall be stronger than the other,
>   the elder shall serve the younger."

24 When her time to give birth was at hand, there were twins in her womb. 25 The first came out red, all his body like a hairy mantle; so they named him Esau.a 26 Afterward his brother came out, with his hand gripping Esau's heel; so he was named Jacob.b Isaac was sixty years old when she bore them.

Heading toward Crisis

27 When the boys grew up, Esau was a skillful hunter, a man of the field, while Jacob was a quiet man, living in tents. 28 Isaac loved Esau, because he was fond of game; but Rebekah loved Jacob.
    29 Once when Jacob was cooking a stew, Esau came in from the field, and he was famished. 30 Esau said to Jacob, "Let me eat some of that red stuff, for I am famished!" (Therefore he was called Edom.c) 31 Jacob said, "First sell me your birthright." 32 Esau said, "I am about to die; of what use is a birthright to me?" 33 Jacob said, "Swear to me first." So he swore to him, and sold his birthright to

---

a The name means "mantled," or "covered"—in this case, with hair.
b That is "He takes by the heel" or "He supplants."
c That is "Red." Esau was regarded as the ancestor of the Edomites, who lived in the south of present-day Jordan.

Jacob. 34 Then Jacob gave Esau bread and lentil stew, and he ate and drank, and rose and went his way. Thus Esau despised his birthright. . . .

26:34 When Esau was forty years old, he married Judith daughter of Beeri the Hittite, and Basemath daughter of Elon the Hittite; 35 and they made life bitter for Isaac and Rebekah.

A Sudden Opportunity

27:1 When Isaac was old and his eyes were dim so that he could not see, he called his elder son Esau and said to him, "My son"; and he answered, "Here I am." 2 He said, "See, I am old; I do not know the day of my death. 3 Now then, take your weapons, your quiver and your bow, and go out to the field, and hunt game for me. 4 Then prepare for me savory food, such as I like, and bring it to me to eat, so that I may bless you before I die."

5 Now Rebekah was listening when Isaac spoke to his son Esau. So when Esau went to the field to hunt for game and bring it, 6 Rebekah said to her son Jacob, "I heard your father say to your brother Esau, 7 'Bring me game, and prepare for me savory food to eat, that I may bless you before the LORD before I die.' 8 Now therefore, my son, obey my word as I command you. 9 Go to the flock, and get me two choice kids, so that I may prepare from them savory food for your father, such as he likes; 10 and you shall take it to your father to eat, so that he may bless you before he dies." 11 But Jacob said to his mother Rebekah, "Look, my brother Esau is a hairy man, and I am a man of smooth skin. 12 Perhaps my father will feel me, and I shall seem to be mocking him, and bring a curse on myself and not a blessing." 13 His mother said to him, "Let your curse be on me, my son; only obey my word, and go, get them for me." 14 So he went and got them and brought them to his mother; and his mother prepared savory food, such as his father loved. 15 Then Rebekah took the best garments of her elder son Esau, which were with her in the house, and put them on her younger son Jacob; 16 and she put the skins of the kids on his hands and on the smooth part of his neck. 17 Then she handed the savory food, and the bread that she had prepared, to her son Jacob.

Questions for Careful Reading

10 minutes
Choose questions according to your interest and time.

1 How long were Isaac and Rebekah married before they had children?

2 Esau seems not to value his birthright. What does Jacob value? What does he not value?

3 In 27:7, Rebekah summarizes what Isaac said to Esau (27:2–4). What does she add? What might the addition suggest about the kind of person she is?

4 Locate the references to family relationships in the conversation between Rebekah and Jacob ("my son," "your father," etc.). Are they all necessary? What effect do they create? What similar relationship terms could have been used but are not? What might their absence imply?

5 How well have Rebekah and Jacob considered their plan? What seems likely to happen as a result of their deception?

6 What are the strengths and weaknesses of each member of the family in this story? How is Jacob like his mother?

A Guide to the Reading

If participants have not read this section already, read it aloud. Otherwise go on to "Questions for Application."

25:19–26. If, as would have been normal in the culture, Rebekah was in her teens when she married Isaac, she must be in her thirties when she becomes pregnant for the first time (25:20, 26)—and with twins, no less. No wonder it is a difficult pregnancy.

At first, Isaac and Rebekah seem to be a devout couple. Isaac prays for Rebekah; she consults God (how, we are not told). Rebekah's answer-to-prayer conception suggests that God has great plans for these children. Yet the boys are already pushing each other around in the womb (25:22), and God tells Rebekah to expect trouble between them (25:23). We may wonder whether the infants' innate combativeness reflects some hidden conflict between their pious parents.

The first baby's ruddy complexion would be taken as a sign of his future physical prowess, his hairiness as a token of his lack of refinement. The second baby is born "afterward"—the word seems tongue-in-cheek, for he is born *with* his brother, gripping Esau's heel as though trying to prevent him from getting into the world first. Despite their almost simultaneous births, the boys have entered life in a definite order. Esau is the firstborn, a position that grants him certain privileges and responsibilities in the society of the time.

25:27–28. Given the congenital conflict between the sons, we may well fear that the parents' opposing preferences for different sons will bring Isaac and Rebekah into conflict with each other.

25:29–34. "Birthright" refers to the rights and rank of the firstborn son. In the ancient Near East, the oldest son inherited a double share of the family's possessions and became the head of the extended family. The birthright status could be transferred if the eldest son wished to bargain it away to another male relative in return for some immediate gain.

"Let me eat some of that red stuff" is more literally "Let me gulp down some of that red red stuff." The words for "red" and "blood" are similar in Hebrew. Perhaps Esau thinks that Jacob is cooking a blood broth that will give him renewed vitality. The words "ate," "drank," "rose," "went his way," and "despised" follow in rapid succession. Biblical scholar Nahum Sarna remarks that the verbal staccato reproduces "the chilling, sullen atmosphere in which Esau silently devours the meal." The stew turns out to have consisted of red lentils rather than anything magical or exotic. Esau has indeed valued his birthright lightly.

26:34–35. The bad light in which Esau stands grows worse still. He has not waited for his parents to arrange a marriage for him, as would have been normal in his society. Even worse, the women he has married give his parents a hard time. Since Isaac by this time is at least a hundred years old (see 25:26 and 26:34), Rebekah may be contemplating the possibility of life as a widow. In the culture of the time, a widow was dependent on her adult sons. Rebekah can hardly welcome the prospect of having to depend on Esau, whose wives are difficult to get along with.

27:1–17. Apparently the father's blessing was separate from the birthright, for even though Esau has relinquished his birthright, he expects to receive Isaac's blessing. The father's blessing of the older son was a kind of sacramental act that channeled God's gift of fertility and God's provision of all that is needed for abundant life (see page 20). Since this blessing designated the recipient as the one who would exercise authority over the extended family (27:29), it could be given only to one son. And since it became effective as the father pronounced it, once spoken it could not be withdrawn. The blessing ceremony customarily included a meal. Nevertheless, the focus on food here (27:4, 7, 9, 14) draws an implicit parallel between Isaac and Esau. Both seem to be excessively concerned with eating (notice the reason why Isaac favors Esau—25:28).

Rebekah seems to have no doubt that Jacob is well qualified for the task of deceiving his father, which suggests something about his character before this incident. His dark side is in full view in his response to his mother's suggestion. His objection is merely "I shall seem to be mocking him" or "I will seem to him to be a trickster." He has no problem with the idea of exploiting his father's blindness. His only concern is whether it can be done successfully.

Rebekah realizes that there is no time to lose standing around debating (27:13). They must act before Esau returns.

Questions for Application

40 minutes
Choose questions according to your interest and time.

1 Reread 25:28. Do parents who have more than one child inevitably favor one of them? What are the results of parental favoritism? What should parents do if they feel a tendency to favor one child?

2 Can rivalry between siblings be avoided? Is it always bad?

3 What religious beliefs and practices protect spouses from destructive conflict with each other? What additional factors are necessary for a husband and wife to grow in unity and love?

4 Do the members of this family respect one another? What difference does respect (or lack of respect) make in family relationships?

5 What are the dangers of acting impetuously? How can a person tell whether quick and decisive action is imprudent or wise?

6 Are you surprised that the Bible contains a story of selfish maneuvering and deception such as this one? What does its presence suggest about the kind of book the Bible is?

7 For personal reflection: Jacob could very well have thought that life had been unfair to him. With some slight repositioning in the womb, he would have been born first and would have lived his entire life as the elder son. Jacob might also have felt that his father was unfair to him: a difference in their personalities made him the less-favored son (25:28). When you were growing up, what aspects of your family relationships seemed less than ideal or even unfair? In what ways did your family background put you at a disadvantage in becoming who you wanted to be? Were your desires for your relationship with your parents frustrated? How have you dealt with these experiences? What constructive ways have you discovered for responding to them?

The starting line for Bible study is not so much a matter of how much a person knows about the Bible as it is of faith in the Bible as the word of God and especially faith in the living, loyal God who speaks these words.

Carroll Stuhlmueller, C.P., "Adult Bible Study: Norms and Goals," *New Theology Review*

Approach to Prayer

15 minutes
Use this approach—or create your own!

♦ Use this time to pray for
families. Begin with an Our
Father. Allow time for silent
prayer and for any petitions that
participants would like to voice
for their own and other families.
End by praying together these
words, adapted from a prayer for
families by Pope John Paul II:

May St. Joseph always guard,
protect, and enlighten
families.
May the Virgin Mary, who is
the mother of the Church,
also be the mother of "the
Church of the home."
May Christ the Lord be present
in every home, bestowing
light, joy, serenity, and
strength.
May every family generously
make its own contribution
to the coming of his
kingdom in the world—a
kingdom of truth and life,
of holiness and grace, of
justice, love, and peace.

Saints in the Making

Problems beneath the Surface

This section is a supplement for individual reading.

Beneath the peaceful surface of their marriage, Isaac and Rebekah were at odds with each other. Their story spurred one husband (who prefers to remain anonymous) to offer this reflection on his own marriage:

In the early years of our marriage, Cheryl and I probably looked like a happy couple. I was a successful small businessman. We had wonderful children. We went to church. We seemed to have it together. But actually, Cheryl and I were locked into a lot of suppressed conflicts.

The biggest area of tension was our finances. At that time, I was the one who earned the money and did the financial planning. It was *my* budget, which I imposed on Cheryl. Eventually, she began purposely overspending just to spite me—as I learned from her later.

Through a series of unexpected incidents, both of us had a significant conversion to Christ. Soon afterward, a downturn in my business brought us into financial difficulties.

One Sunday night, we made a decision to talk about our finances after the children had gone to sleep. I showed up at the kitchen table with my budget, calculator, and yellow tablet. But before I started talking, we were led by the Spirit to kneel down on the kitchen floor together and ask the Lord for help. Then I sat quietly and let Cheryl talk first and did not interrupt.

I was astounded to learn that she was *not* against me and, further, that she had some really good ideas about how we could make our finances work better. She had several suggestions that proved revolutionary: first, that we meet like this twice a month before each of my paychecks to plan how to spend that infusion of money; second, that we use a priority system to manage our money. The third thing was that neither of us would ever spend more than we had decided we would without the other's consent.

Looking back thirty years later, I can honestly say we experienced this conversation as a major work of God, using the grace of the sacrament of matrimony. Not only did we begin working *together* on our finances for the first time, but our steps in the area of finances brought us into peace in other areas of our life also. God set us on the path of becoming more unselfish and loving toward each other.

Between Discussions

Well, That's a Blessing

As Isaac rests on his bed and Esau crouches in wait for a gazelle and Rebekah hands the savory dish to Jacob and Jacob steps to the entrance of his father's tent, all are thinking of one thing: the blessing. The father's blessing is the center of attention. What is this blessing?

We may be familiar with blessings in the Church today, but the concept of blessing has undergone much development in the biblical and Christian traditions. To grasp the meaning of the blessing that Isaac is about to give, we need to make some distinctions between our present Catholic concept of blessing and the concept in Genesis.

The Catholic idea of blessing is expressed in part, at least, in the familiar prayer before meals: "Bless us, O Lord, and these thy gifts, which we are about to receive from thy bounty, through Christ our Lord. Amen." In this prayer we ask God to bless us and the food, that is, to use the meal to nourish and strengthen us—and to see that it does us no harm!—so that we might live in his love and peace.

Isaac and his family also connected blessing with nourishment, strength, and peace. But they would have thought it odd to ask God to bless the food. Food, they would have said, *is* God's blessing. To their way of thinking, blessing is the gift of life: blessing consists of the power of fertility, of the natural forces that bring growth, of the circumstances that yield prosperity and success.

This view of blessing is displayed in the first chapter of the Bible. At creation, God "blessed" the living creatures of the earth (1:22), giving them the capacity to reproduce. Turning to humankind, God "blessed" them with these words: "Be fruitful and multiply, and fill the earth . . . and have dominion over the fish . . . over the birds . . . and over every living thing . . ." (1:28). God granted humans "every plant yielding seed" and "every tree with seed in its fruit" (1:29). This creation blessing was not a special divine wish that everything would go well for people. The blessing was the life and procreative potential he granted human beings, along with the earth as a life-sustaining environment.

The Bible shows that the first humans passed on this original blessing to their children. Those boring genealogies in Genesis, listing generation after generation (see especially Genesis 5:2–3 and the listing that follows it), are actually descriptions of the high-voltage cables through which the current of God's blessing was transmitted from the first humans to the human race in the present day.

In Isaac and Rebekah's culture, people believed that parents first handed on God's blessing to their children in the very act of love that brings conception. From parents the child receives life—the essence of all blessing! The parents then continue to bless their children by providing them with the resources that will enable them to live full lives. This ongoing blessing of their children involves providing them with food, shelter, protection, education, and tools— and also conveying to them an attitude of trust in God. The parental transfer of God-given life to the next generation culminates in a solemn ceremony in which the father prays that God will provide the eldest son (this was a patriarchal culture) with the inner vitality and favorable circumstances necessary for him to lead the family into well-being. This is the blessing at the center of our story.

This final blessing took place near the end of the father's life. The oldest son brought his father special food, thus helping the father to summon his diminishing life forces for the completion of the transfer of the blessing. Thus Isaac tells Esau to bring him his special dish, "so that I may bless you" (27:4; see also 27:19, 25, 31); more literally the Hebrew reads "so that my soul—my life force—may bless you." The father passed on the blessing he had received from God. God, not the father, is the source of blessing (27:28).

In the view of people in Isaac and Rebekah's culture, this fatherly blessing has a kind of sacramental effectiveness. It reliably conveys God's creation blessing. Once transmitted, the blessing is irrevocable. While accepting the view that humans are the channel of God's blessing to one another, however, the narrator of our story will invite us to question whether humans can control and limit the flow of God's blessings.

WHO ARE YOU, MY SON?

Questions to Begin

15 minutes
Use a question or two to get warmed up for the reading.

1 If you could order anything you wished for dinner tomorrow night, what would it be?

2 What is the longest you've ever waited to be served in a restaurant?

5 minutes
Read the passage aloud. Let individuals take turns reading
paragraphs.

The Reading: Genesis 27:18–45

Deception

18 So he went in to his father, and said, "My father"; and he said,
"Here I am; who are you, my son?" 19 Jacob said to his father, "I am
Esau your firstborn. I have done as you told me; now sit up and eat
of my game, so that you may bless me." 20 But Isaac said to his son,
"How is it that you have found it so quickly, my son?" He answered,
"Because the LORD your God granted me success." 21 Then Isaac
said to Jacob, "Come near, that I may feel you, my son, to know
whether you are really my son Esau or not." 22 So Jacob went up to
his father Isaac, who felt him and said, "The voice is Jacob's voice,
but the hands are the hands of Esau." 23 He did not recognize him,
because his hands were hairy like his brother Esau's hands; so he
blessed him. 24 He said, "Are you really my son Esau?" He answered,
"I am." 25 Then he said, "Bring it to me, that I may eat of my son's
game and bless you." So he brought it to him, and he ate; and he
brought him wine, and he drank. 26 Then his father Isaac said to
him, "Come near and kiss me, my son." 27 So he came near and
kissed him; and he smelled the smell of his garments, and blessed
him, and said,

> "Ah, the smell of my son
>   is like the smell of a field that the LORD has blessed.
> 28 May God give you of the dew of heaven,
>   and of the fatness of the earth,
>   and plenty of grain and wine.
> 29 Let peoples serve you,
>   and nations bow down to you.
> Be lord over your brothers,
>   and may your mother's sons bow down to you.
> Cursed be everyone who curses you,
>   and blessed be everyone who blesses you!"

30 As soon as Isaac had finished blessing Jacob, when Jacob
had scarcely gone out from the presence of his father Isaac, his
brother Esau came in from his hunting. 31 He also prepared savory
food, and brought it to his father. And he said to his father, "Let my
father sit up and eat of his son's game, so that you may bless me."

32 His father Isaac said to him, "Who are you?" He answered, "I am your firstborn son, Esau." 33 Then Isaac trembled violently, and said, "Who was it then that hunted game and brought it to me, and I ate it all before you came, and I have blessed him?—yes, and blessed he shall be!" 34 When Esau heard his father's words, he cried out with an exceedingly great and bitter cry, and said to his father, "Bless me, me also, father!" 35 But he said, "Your brother came deceitfully, and he has taken away your blessing." 36 Esau said, "Is he not rightly named Jacob?ª For he has supplanted me these two times. He took away my birthright; and look, now he has taken away my blessing." Then he said, "Have you not reserved a blessing for me?" 37 Isaac answered Esau, "I have already made him your lord, and I have given him all his brothers as servants, and with grain and wine I have sustained him. What then can I do for you, my son?" 38 Esau said to his father, "Have you only one blessing, father? Bless me, me also, father!" And Esau lifted up his voice and wept.

39 Then his father Isaac answered him:

> "See, away from the fatness of the earth shall your
> home be,
> and away from the dew of heaven on high.
> 40 By your sword you shall live,
> and you shall serve your brother;
> but when you break loose,
> you shall break his yoke from your neck."

41 Now Esau hated Jacob because of the blessing with which his father had blessed him, and Esau said to himself, "The days of mourning for my father are approaching; then I will kill my brother Jacob." 42 But the words of her elder son Esau were told to Rebekah; so she sent and called her younger son Jacob and said to him, "Your brother Esau is consoling himself by planning to kill you. 43 Now therefore, my son, obey my voice; flee at once to my brother Laban in Haran, 44 and stay with him a while, until your brother's fury turns away—45 until your brother's anger against you turns away, and he forgets what you have done to him; then I will send, and bring you back from there. Why should I lose both of you in one day?"

ª That is "He supplants" or "He takes by the heel."

10 minutes
Choose questions according to your interest and time.

1 How many lies does Jacob tell? Does he tell the truth at all?

2 How many of the Ten Commandments (Exodus 20:1–17) does Jacob violate in this scene?

3 Why doesn't Esau answer the question that Isaac asks in verse 33?

4 Reread verse 33. Has Isaac fully realized at this point the extent of the deception to which he has fallen victim? What picture of Isaac do you draw from what we've read so far?

5 Why does the narrator keep identifying Isaac as "his father" (27:22, 26, 30, 32, and 39)?

6 In 27:45, who is Rebekah afraid of losing? Does it seem likely that she can avoid the loss she fears?

A Guide to the Reading

*If participants have not read this section already, read it aloud.
Otherwise go on to "Questions for Application."*

27:18–29. Jacob addresses his father as briefly as possible
(27:18; in Hebrew, "my father" is a single word). Is he hesitant,
waiting to see if his deception is going to work? In any case, his
greeting of "my father" underlines the almost sacrilegious nature
of the deception he is about to perpetrate. Jacob is preparing
to deceive the one who has given him life—and who is about to
complete this gift of life with a final blessing.

Isaac has only two sons, so his question "Who are you,
my son?" can only mean "Which son are you?" Does Isaac, like
Rebekah, instinctively know that Jacob is a deceiver?

Perhaps sensing that the old man is already half convinced,
Jacob boldly asserts that he has carried out his father's wishes.
What irony!

Since the tasty dish called for game, which had to be
caught, it would take time to prepare. But Rebekah and Jacob
have to hurry to get the meal to Isaac before Esau returns. Not
surprisingly, the speedy appearance of the tray of food arouses
Isaac's suspicions. "How on earth did you ever find it so quickly?"
he asks.

Knowing that Isaac is a pious man, who believes that God
answers prayers (25:21), Jacob shamelessly attributes his speedy
arrival to God's help (27:20). "Dad, it was just like you've so often
said: With God, all things are possible!" Significantly, Jacob tells
his father, "Your God granted me success." Apparently Jacob is not
worried about his father's God protecting his father from treachery.

"Are you really my son Esau?" Isaac asks again (see 27:24).
The old man cannot shake the suspicion that Jacob is deceiving
him, but he seems reluctant to accuse him. Finally, convinced by
stolen evidence—Esau's clothing—Isaac gives Jacob his blessing.
In the process, Isaac expresses his delight with Esau (27:27). Is this
the paternal favor that Jacob has long desired to experience?

27:30–40. Jacob was born a second too late to be the
older brother. Now Esau arrives a second too late to prevent the
theft of his blessing. Esau's failure to notice that his dress clothes
are missing implies that he is in such a hurry to get back to his
father that he does not pause to change. His disregard for such

niceties is in keeping with his rough personality. It also suggests how eager he is to receive his father's blessing.

Esau's longer greeting (27:31) contrasts with Jacob's single word. Esau has no reason to be guarded. "Who are you?" Isaac responds. He does not ask, "Who are you, my son?" (compare with 27:18), for he is sure that he has given his blessing to Esau, and this second voice is certainly not Jacob's.

As soon as Esau identifies himself (27:32), Isaac knows that he has been tricked. But could Jacob, his own son, really have done such a thing? Esau ignores Isaac's question. His first thought is not to accuse Jacob but to wrest a blessing from his father. Boorish Esau didn't seem to give a second thought to relinquishing his birthright, but the loss of his father's blessing grieves him deeply. Perhaps he places a higher value on his father's love than on his father's possessions. He certainly places a higher value on his father than Jacob does.

Isaac's blessing of Esau is ambiguous. The Hebrew of verse 39 may mean that Esau will *live apart from* the fertile agricultural areas or that he will *derive some benefit from* the fertile lands. The region of the Edomites—Esau's descendants—included some fertile land as well as much wilderness.

27:41–45. Rebekah is again quick to devise a plan. She tells Jacob that she is afraid of losing "both of you in one day." Perhaps she means that on the day Isaac dies, she will lose Jacob also, for Esau will kill him—although we may wonder whether she would regard the death of Isaac as any great loss. Or she may mean that she fears that if Esau murders Jacob, other relatives will kill Esau in revenge, and thus she will lose both her sons—but, again, we may wonder how much Rebekah would regret Esau's death. And hasn't she in fact lost all three men in her life in a single blow?

Only in these final words does Rebekah speak in terms of her own advantage. Jacob (and the reader) looks into Rebekah's face and suddenly understands whose interests have been uppermost in her mind all along.

Questions for Application

40 minutes
Choose questions according to your interest and time.

---

1 Have you ever grasped for something in a way that caused harm to other people—and to yourself?

---

2 When can a blessing turn out to be a curse? Can a blessing contain a hidden disadvantage? What has been your experience with this?

---

3 Personality strengths sometimes have corresponding weaknesses. A person's vices sometimes have corresponding virtues. What might be the corresponding good points of someone who is artful at deceiving others? What might be the strengths of someone like Esau?

4 What advice would you offer each of the characters at this point in the story? (What are the dangers of offering advice to people in situations like this?)

5 For personal reflection: In the story of Isaac and Rebekah and their sons, the narrator avoids whitewashing the characters' flaws and failings. This is characteristic of the Bible, which generally deals unsparingly with people's sins. How straightforward are you with yourself about your own sins?

Making connections between events in the Scriptures and situations in my own life was my first exciting breakthrough in Bible study. That's when the Word came alive for me.

Kitty Rodgers, "Can Bible Study Really Change Your Life?" *New Theology Review*

Approach to Prayer

15 minutes
Use this approach—or create your own!

♦ Let one participant pray the following prayer aloud for the group. After a moment of silent reflection, allow time for spontaneous, short prayers, if any wish to offer them. End with an Our Father.

O God, in various ways—you know them so well—we have polluted the environment of our families, our friendships, and our working relationships with deception, selfishness, pride, and refusal to forgive. In some of our relationships, the soil has become poisoned; the flowers of peace and joy have become rare or nonexistent. Nevertheless, Lord, "When you send forth your spirit . . . you renew the face of the ground."[a] And so we ask you, Lord, to send the cleansing rain of your Spirit upon us, to give us the grace of repentance and reconciliation. Restore our damaged relationships. Restore our hearts.

[a] Psalm 104:30

A Living Tradition
Jacob vs. Esau

This section is a supplement for individual reading.

In a long tradition of interpretation, Jews and Christians have viewed the conflict between Jacob and Esau from different angles and have given it various applications.

For centuries in the Old Testament period, the story of Jacob and Esau provided the Israelites with background for their geopolitical situation. They regarded themselves as the descendants of Jacob. They saw his brother, Esau, as the ancestor of the Edomites—a neighboring people who lived in what is now southern Jordan.

The Israelites and the Edomites were chronically at each other's throats. In their region, to the east of the Dead Sea, the Edomites dominated a major trade route that was a valuable source of revenue—a trade route that the Israelites wished to make their own. To the west, the Israelites tried to develop the copper deposits in the Negev desert. But the Edomites, who lived closer to the copper mines than the Israelites did, challenged their control of the mines.

King David conquered the Edomites, and his successors held them as vassals. Eventually the Edomites freed themselves and took revenge on the Israelites. When the Babylonians captured the Israelite capital, Jerusalem, in 587 B.C., the Edomites looked on with satisfaction; then they took advantage of the Israelites' vulnerability and attacked them. An entire prophetic book, Obadiah, is devoted to a bitter denunciation of this Edomite aggression—lasting testimony to the hatred that had developed between the two peoples.

In the midst of this conflict, the story of Jacob and Esau reminded the Israelites that their Edomite enemies were, nevertheless, their brethren. Moses had instructed the Israelites, "You shall not abhor any of the Edomites, for they are your kin" (Deuteronomy 23:7).

Biblical scholar Claus Westermann points out that although the conflict between the Israelites and the Edomites ended long ago, we can still learn a lesson from this biblical recognition of kinship between warring nations. It reminds us that "every war is in essence a war between brothers."

The first generation of Christians confronted a troubling situation. The Christian mission among the Jews achieved some early success but then ran into increasing resistance. Jesus, the Messiah of the Jews, was not recognized as such by most of the Jewish people. Before long, the majority of men and women entering the Christian community were gentiles. For Jewish Christians, this was a shocking, unexpected development. How could such an illogical situation have occurred?

St. Paul pondered this problem in his letter to the Romans (chapters 9 through 11). Without denying human freedom, Paul noted that people's acceptance of the gospel is a matter of responding to God's call, and God freely chooses those whom he calls to himself. Paul concluded that the limited response to the gospel among the Jewish people somehow reflected a mysterious divine plan. Paul made no claim that human beings can understand this plan, although he gave examples of how God's plan works for what is best. For instance, in some sense the failure of most Jews to acknowledge Jesus as the Messiah opened the way for other people to receive the gospel.

To demonstrate how inscrutable God's choosing of people is, Paul cited the story of Jacob and Esau. Before either of them was born, before they did anything that might have won or lost them God's approval, God chose Jacob to be the one through whom his promises to the family of Abraham would be transmitted to the next generation. God persisted in his choice of Jacob, even when Jacob displayed a seriously flawed character. Paul writes that after Rebekah conceived the boys, the Lord told her that the elder would serve the younger. "What then are we to say?" Paul asked. "Is there injustice on God's part? By no means! For he says to Moses, 'I will have mercy on whom I have mercy, and I will have compassion on whom I have compassion'" (Romans 9:11–15).

The early Christian teachers—often called the Church Fathers—used this comparison of Jacob and Esau with Christians and Jews as a key for interpreting the story in the book of Genesis. That is to say, Paul's words led the Church Fathers to view the conflict between Jacob and Esau as a prophetic allegory of the conflict between Christians and Jews that the Church Fathers experienced in their own day.

This approach to the account in Genesis, however, involves explaining away Jacob's dishonest behavior. Speaking of the Church Fathers' approach, a modern scholar remarks, "One admires the indulgence with which our authors interpret the ruses of the patriarch so as to see nothing more than the accomplishment of the will of God." Jacob's deceptions were by the "arrangement of providence," St. John Chrysostom asserted. St. Augustine interpreted the animal skins that Jacob wore to fool Isaac as an image of humankind's sins borne by Christ. Jacob's untruthful words to his father were "not a lie but a mystery," Augustine wrote. (Yet not every Church Father concurred in this line of interpretation. St. Jerome frankly acknowledged that Jacob lied.)

Whatever value the Fathers' indulgent approach may have, it has a significant weakness: It obscures the primary sense of the story, which recounts how Jacob sinned against his father and brother. By making Jacob's sin less prominent, the Fathers' approach makes God's graciousness to Jacob seem less remarkable.

Another way of viewing the conflict between Esau and Jacob, called the "moral interpretation," began with the Church Fathers and became popular during the Middle Ages. In this way of reading the story, Jacob is viewed as an image of growth in the spiritual life, while Esau is taken to be an image of failure to aspire to higher goods. Jacob is such a model, medieval writers argued, because he "overcame nature," that is, despite being the younger son, he gained the inheritance that would naturally have gone to his older brother. Overcoming nature, of course, is what all of us must do in the Christian life, in the sense of curbing our darker drives in order to love God and others. By contrast, Esau, because he preferred a bowl of stew to his birthright as an heir of God's promises to Abraham, is an image of being fixated on earthly satisfactions to the neglect of higher things.

From the point of view of the moral interpretation, Jacob and Esau represent contrary tendencies within each of us. As the ninth-century writer Claude de Turin put it, "Two nations and two peoples are within us," struggling for mastery. In that sense, we are all pregnant Rebekahs.

Between Discussions

So Many Questions

A story that started out looking like it could be entitled "A Nice Couple and Their Two Promising Boys" has turned into a tale that could better be called "Mother and Son Wreck a Family." Ancient Near Eastern families were bound tightly by cultural expectations and economic necessity. In a shepherding family everyone shared the work and the rewards of caring for the livestock. Yet even a close-knit family like Isaac and Rebekah's could be torn apart if individual members set their own interests against the interests of others. In the case of this family, Jacob takes advantage of Esau's hunger. Esau disregards his parents' wishes by bringing into the extended family wives who make life difficult for them. Isaac favors Esau, apparently because he takes pleasure in his son's outdoor interests—and in the game he brings back. Rebekah and Jacob play Isaac for a fool in order to wrest a position in the family away from Esau. Rebekah, it seems, manipulates Jacob in order to ensure for herself a more comfortable widowhood.

The story, then, raises a question about the vulnerability and reparability of family life. Evidently the bonds of custom and economics are not enough to keep this family together in the face of the individual members' pursuit of selfish agendas—a pursuit that seems to come naturally to everyone in the family, young and old. Is there any resource that can counterbalance family members' centrifugal tendencies? If a family begins to disintegrate, can anything put it back together?

Our reading also raises a question concerning cleverness. Isaac and Esau are unperceptive, easily manipulated. By contrast, Rebekah and Jacob are quick-witted; they instinctively size up a situation and know how to take advantage of it. By the end of the episode, however, Rebekah and Jacob are looking less clever than they did a little earlier. Esau is planning to murder Jacob, and Rebekah is advising Jacob to flee. She tells Jacob, "Now therefore, my son, obey my voice" (27:43). In the Hebrew, her words precisely echo her words to him when she first laid out her plan (27:8). That plan, it is now obvious, was ill-conceived. Will her plan for damage control work any better? How long will "a while" be (27:44)? In cooking up her original scheme, Rebekah did not take into account Esau's reaction. Has she yet recognized the full depth of his anger? She thinks he will soon forget. But will Esau's fury ever turn away from his brother? Is Rebekah and Jacob's kind of cleverness truly clever?

Other questions concern Jacob in particular. He has stolen a blessing. Will he now be blessed? Can God be tricked into giving his gifts? Blessing—the power of life, fertility, and success—comes from God. How can Jacob truly be blessed if he is not connected to God? (Does Jacob have any relationship with God? Consider "your God"—27:20.) Specifically, Isaac's blessing envisions Jacob experiencing the bounty of farm and flocks. Will he? Under what circumstances? Isaac has put Jacob at the head of the family. But how can Jacob exercise a protective, fostering leadership over a family that he himself has torn apart by deception and theft? Now that he has shown himself unworthy of trust, how can anyone in the family trust him to lead them?

Jacob has treated both God and his father with contempt. His answer to Isaac's question about how he found the game so quickly—"The Lord your God granted me success" (27:20)—is almost blasphemous. Are there no consequences for treating God—and other people—with such scorn?

Rebekah and Jacob's stratagem for displacing Esau may remind us of an earlier incident in which a man and woman decided to grab for something in a way that violated God's law (Genesis 3). It seems that the drama in the garden of Eden is replayed over and over in human life, including family life.

After Adam and Eve ate the forbidden fruit, God revealed to them the painful consequences of their actions but also treated them kindly. Will God act redemptively toward Rebekah and Jacob also?

If you keep these questions in mind as you read the rest of the story, you will find answers.

DIVINE APPOINTMENTS

Questions to Begin

15 minutes
Use a question or two to get warmed up for the reading.

---

1 How do you respond when someone tells you, "I had the weirdest dream last night"?
☐ I'm all ears—the stranger the better.
☐ I'm always eager to try my hand at dream interpretation.
☐ I seize the first opportunity to recount my own dreams.
☐ I tell them it was something they ate.
☐ Let me out!

---

2 What's the highest you've ever climbed? How do you react to heights?

---

3 Have you ever visited a shrine or gone on a pilgrimage? What did you get out of it?

5 minutes
Read the passage aloud. Let individuals take turns reading
paragraphs.

The Reading: Genesis 27:46–28:5; 28:10–29:14

Rebekah's Last Ruse

27:46 Then Rebekah said to Isaac, "I am weary of my life because of
the Hittite women. If Jacob marries one of the Hittite women such as
these, one of the women of the land, what good will my life be to me?"
        28:1 Then Isaac called Jacob and blessed him, and charged
him, "You shall not marry one of the Canaanite women. 2 Go at
once to Paddan-aram to the house of Bethuel, your mother's father;
and take as wife from there one of the daughters of Laban, your
mother's brother. 3 May God Almighty bless you and make you
fruitful and numerous, that you may become a company of peoples.
4 May he give to you the blessing of Abraham, to you and to your
offspring with you, so that you may take possession of the land
where you now live as an alien—land that God gave to Abraham."
5 Thus Isaac sent Jacob away. . . .

A Stairway to Heaven

10 Jacob left Beer-sheba and went toward Haran. 11 He came to a
certain place and stayed there for the night, because the sun had set.
Taking one of the stones of the place, he put it under his head and lay
down in that place. 12 And he dreamed that there was a ladder set up
on the earth, the top of it reaching to heaven; and the angels of God
were ascending and descending on it. 13 And the LORD stood beside
him and said, "I am the LORD, the God of Abraham your father and
the God of Isaac; the land on which you lie I will give to you and
to your offspring; 14 and your offspring shall be like the dust of the
earth, and you shall spread abroad to the west and to the east and to
the north and to the south; and all the families of the earth shall be
blessed in you and in your offspring. 15 Know that I am with you and
will keep you wherever you go, and will bring you back to this land;
for I will not leave you until I have done what I have promised you."
16 Then Jacob woke from his sleep and said, "Surely the LORD is in
this place—and I did not know it!" 17 And he was afraid, and said,
"How awesome is this place! This is none other than the house of
God, and this is the gate of heaven."

18 So Jacob rose early in the morning, and he took the stone that he had put under his head and set it up for a pillar and poured oil on the top of it. 19 He called that place Bethela. . . . 20 Then Jacob made a vow, saying, "If God will be with me, and will keep me in this way that I go, and will give me bread to eat and clothing to wear, 21 so that I come again to my father's house in peace, then the LORD shall be my God, 22 and this stone, which I have set up for a pillar, shall be God's house; and of all that you give me I will surely give one tenth to you."

A Promising Start

29:1 Then Jacob went on his journey, and came to the land of the people of the east. 2 As he looked, he saw a well in the field and three flocks of sheep lying there beside it; for out of that well the flocks were watered. The stone on the well's mouth was large, 3 and when all the flocks were gathered there, the shepherds would roll the stone from the mouth of the well, and water the sheep. . . .

4 Jacob said to them, "My brothers, where do you come from?" They said, "We are from Haran." 5 He said to them, "Do you know Laban son of Nahor?" They said, "We do." 6 He said to them, "Is it well with him?" "Yes," they replied, "and here is his daughter Rachel, coming with the sheep." . . .

9 While he was still speaking with them, Rachel came with her father's sheep; for she kept them. 10 Now when Jacob saw Rachel, the daughter of his mother's brother Laban, and the sheep of his mother's brother Laban, Jacob went up and rolled the stone from the well's mouth, and watered the flock of his mother's brother Laban. 11 Then Jacob kissed Rachel, and wept aloud. 12 And Jacob told Rachel that he was her father's kinsman, and that he was Rebekah's son; and she ran and told her father.

13 When Laban heard the news about his sister's son Jacob, he ran to meet him; he embraced him and kissed him, and brought him to his house. Jacob told Laban all these things, 14 and Laban said to him, "Surely you are my bone and my flesh!" And he stayed with him a month.

a That is "The House of God."

10 minutes
Choose questions according to your interest and time.

1 Why does Rebekah complain about the "Hittite women" (27:46; see 26:34–35)? Why does she mention them now? What does the tone of Rebekah's complaint reveal about her?

2 How and why is Isaac's direction to Jacob (28:1–2) different from the advice Rebekah has already given him (27:43–45)? How long does each of the parents expect their son to be away?

3 Does Isaac's farewell blessing (28:3–4) add anything to what Jacob already received in 27:27–29? What does the scene suggest about Isaac's state of mind?

4 What is surprising about Jacob's dream? Does Jacob's reaction to it fit with your picture of him? What seems in character? What does not?

5 See 29:13. How much of the "things" that had happened do you think Jacob told Laban?

A Guide to the Reading

If participants have not read this section already, read it aloud. Otherwise go on to "Questions for Application."

27:46–28:5. Isaac seems blind to Rebekah's new deception and to the murder threat hanging over Jacob. Intent on keeping him that way, Rebekah voices a melodramatic complaint about Esau's wives. A model for manipulators, it is an indirect rebuke that creates anxiety and nudges Isaac into unwittingly activating Rebekah's getaway plan for Jacob (27:43–45).

Isaac obligingly instructs Jacob to go find a bride from among Rebekah's nieces in Mesopotamia (28:2). Though he is really a fugitive, Jacob gets a ceremonial sendoff and a blessing that clearly identifies him as the next heir to God's promises to Abraham (17:1–8; 26:2–4). Is Isaac resigned to Esau's displacement? Maybe it has hit him that he himself inherited Abraham's blessing at the expense of his elder half brother, Ishmael (17:18–21).

We imagine Rebekah waving a stoic goodbye to her coddled son. It is her last view of him—and our last view of her.

28:10–15. Jacob's perilous 500–mile trek from Beersheba to Haran is undescribed except for one life-changing encounter. Significantly, it happens when Jacob is asleep and at his most helpless. Like infrared lenses that make visible what lies in darkness, his dream reveals the reality behind appearances: He is neither alone nor the master of his destiny.

Jacob finds himself near a celestial thoroughfare, with God's servants moving up and down a lofty "ladder set up on the earth" (28:12). The more literal translation—"placed toward the earth"— suggests that this stairway is a divine initiative, something let down from heaven, not a human construct like the Tower of Babel, built up from the earth (11:4). We can know God not because we can rise to his level by our unaided powers but because he chooses to reveal himself to us.

It is not clear in the Hebrew whether Jacob sees the Lord standing "beside" him (an image of God's intimate presence in the ordinary) or "above" him (suggesting God's sovereign rule over heaven and earth). Either way, the runaway who managed to elude his angry brother has run right into his father's God (27:20).

Astonishingly, God does not rebuke Jacob but offers him promises that fly in the face of circumstances. Jacob is heading into exile, is unmarried, and is unskilled at fostering a harmonious family life. This unpromising specimen will nonetheless possess the land, have numerous children, and bless "all the families of the earth" (28:13–14). Additionally, he receives a guarantee of safe-conduct and right of return (28:15). Wisely, the narrator of Jacob's story does not try to justify God's approach. Biblical scholar Gerhard von Rad observes, "No art of empathy can succeed in understanding the incomprehensible, namely, that the fleeing deceiver received such a word of grace."

28:16–22. To his credit, Jacob is amazed too. Perhaps sensing the disparity between divine mercy and his behavior, he is "afraid," profoundly shaken by the mystery of God's presence (28:17). He memorializes the event by setting up a monument. Such stone pillars were often several feet high—our first inkling that tent-dwelling Jacob is not necessarily a physical weakling.

The sour note in Jacob's response is the "if" clause in his vow (28:20–22). Why are all the conditions placed on God, when God has just *promised* he will do these very things? The wary bargainer seems unready to commit himself.

29:1–14. Jacob's new life as a convert-in-process kicks off with a flurry of divine appointments that underline God's mysterious blessing. Not only does the traveler happen on the right territory, field, and well, but he also arrives just as his bride-to-be approaches. In the very setting where Rebekah was discovered as the right bride for Isaac (Genesis 24), Jacob meets Rachel. Their family connection is repeatedly mentioned (29:10, 12, 13, 14). This functions as a flashing neon sign telling Jacob, "This is the woman for you!" (28:2). It could also be a warning that relatives of Rebekah may share some of her problematic tendencies.

Immediately smitten, Jacob responds to Rachel with a display of physical prowess, physical labor, and physical affection (29:10–11). Is he similarly unguarded in recounting "all these things" to Laban (29:13)? Or does he pass over his deception and present himself only as a prospective suitor who has, through some misfortune, arrived penniless? Whatever Uncle Laban hears and sees, he likes it and pronounces Jacob a man after his own heart (29:14).

Questions for Application

40 minutes
Choose questions according to your interest and time.

1 Rebekah feeds Isaac a fake reason for doing what she wants him to do. How do you think such beneath-the-surface maneuverings affect personal relationships?

2 Can you identify times in your own life when God treated you with mercy even though you knew yourself to be especially undeserving? What are some ways of passing God's mercy along to others, especially to "problem" people—including those in your family?

3 Jacob bursts into tears when he meets Rachel (29:11). Probably he is relieved at finding himself among family—no longer a stranger in a strange land. Do you know any "strangers" or estranged members of your family who might experience similar relief if you extended an offer of friendship or hospitality?

4 Do you think Jacob acted prudently when he met Uncle Laban? What is prudence, anyway? (You'll find an explanation in the *Catechism of the Catholic Church*, section 1806.)

5 Have you ever made God a promise? Have you delivered on it? (Don't forget baptismal and confirmation promises and marriage or religious vows!)

6 For personal reflection: Because of the Incarnation, every ordinary part of every ordinary day in this physical universe is a potential "gate of heaven." Do you ever expect to meet the Lord as you go about your everyday duties? Do you look for him in your conversations, your work, your comings and goings? What could you do to develop a greater sense of expectancy and awareness that God is with you in the day's activities? a greater sense of trust even when you do not sense his presence?

Good Bible students ask a lot of questions. Why questions are especially helpful.

Rolf E. Aaseng, *A Beginner's Guide to Studying the Bible*

Approach to Prayer

15 minutes
Use this approach—or create your own!

♦ Consider God's mercy—
especially as revealed in the
life, death, and resurrection
of Jesus. Have someone read
a short Scripture passage
that proclaims God's love and
mercy—perhaps Romans 5:7–8
or 1 John 1:5–9.

After reflecting on ways in
which you have needed and
received God's mercy, express
your thanks by praying or singing
these verses from "Amazing
Grace":

Amazing grace! How sweet the
    sound
That saved a wretch like me!
I once was lost, but now am
    found,
Was blind, but now I see.

'Twas grace that taught my heart
    to fear,
And grace my fears relieved;
How precious did that grace
    appear
The hour I first believed!

Through many dangers, toils,
    and snares
I have already come;
'Tis grace has brought me safe
    thus far,
And grace will lead me home.

A Living Tradition

The Real Ladder to Success

This section is a supplement for individual reading.

Even before a fugitive named Jacob laid himself down with a stone for a pillow, ancient peoples saw the sky as the realm of divine mysteries and sought spiritual encounters by going "up." The Genesis story of Jacob may have been influenced by such traditions. The unusual Hebrew word translated "ladder" (28:12) is a possible reference to the zigzagging outer ramps or flights of stairs on Babylonian temple towers.

For early Christians looking to describe the ascent to God, Jacob's ladder was rich with symbolic meaning. Ladder images figure in the art of the early Christians in Rome. In the gripping account of the death of St. Perpetua, in 203, the young married woman understands that her martyrdom is imminent when, in a dream, she sees herself invited to climb "a golden ladder of marvelous height, reaching up even to heaven, and very narrow."

For the most part, though, Christians seized on Jacob's ladder as a visual invitation to union with God through long-term purification and progress in virtue. In a typical homily, the fourth-century Church Father John Chrysostom urged listeners to take stock of their sins and faults in order to correct them one by one, a month at a time. "In this way, ascending by steps, let us get to heaven by a Jacob's ladder," he said. "Let us undertake this journey so that, having arrived in heaven, we will rejoice in all its blessings."

Over the centuries, more organized help for the vertical pilgrimage came from numerous spiritual writers who proposed variously constructed "ladders" for scaling the heights. Made up of anywhere from 3 to 190 rungs or steps, they usually traced the stages of the climb to God through personal growth in specific virtues. This rich treasury of "ladder" writings includes devotional masterpieces that remain useful and inspiring to this day. Here are just a few—all of them available in modern translations.

The Rule of St. Benedict (sixth century). Chapter 7 of this influential work is an early twelve-step program focused on the key virtue of humility. "We must erect the ladder which appeared to Jacob in his dream," says Benedict. "The erected ladder is our life in the present world, which if the heart is humble, is by the Lord lifted up to heaven." The climb begins with fear of the Lord and ends with "that perfect love of God which casts out fear."

The Ladder of Divine Ascent (seventh century).
Thirty steps—one for each year of Christ's hidden life—make up the
spiritual ascent described by the abbot of Sinai, St. John Climacus
(from the Greek word *klimakos,* meaning "ladder"). Moving from
initial conversion to growth in virtue to union with God, the desert
monk writes with humor, color, and compassion, offering such
realistic advice as a warning not to climb the entire ladder "in a
single stride." For good reason, John's *Ladder* remains the preferred
spiritual reading of many Eastern Christians, holding a place
comparable to that of *The Imitation of Christ* in the West.

Scivias (twelfth century). The image of Jacob's
ladder underlies a vision described in this prophetic work by the
mystic St. Hildegard of Bingen. She speaks of Christ as a "pillar"
containing "an ascent like a ladder from bottom to top" on which not
angels but "all the virtues of God" are traveling. Seven stand out,
charity and humility most outstandingly. Without offering a program,
Hildegard's vision encourages meditation on Jesus, who "left in
himself the way of salvation" so that "faithful people both small and
great can find in him the right step on which to place their foot in
order to ascend to virtue."

The Ladder of Four Rungs (twelfth century).
Composed by a Carthusian known as Guigo II, this short guide to
spiritual growth was written as a letter. Guigo calls it a "ladder for
monks," but any Christian can benefit from his description of its four
rungs of Scripture reading, meditation, prayer, and contemplation.
The ladder is short, says Guigo, "yet its length is immense and
wonderful, for its lower end rests upon the earth but its top pierces
the clouds and touches heavenly secrets."

Other noteworthy offerings in the Christian "ladder"
literature include Elizabeth of Schönau's *Book of the Journey to
God* (twelfth century); St. Bonaventure's *Journey of the Mind to God*
(thirteenth century); Walter Hilton's *Scale of Perfection* (fourteenth
century); St. John of the Cross's *Ascent of Mount Carmel* (sixteenth
century); and St. Robert Bellarmine's *The Mind's Ascent to God by
the Ladder of Created Things* (seventeenth century).

None of these writers intended to leave their audiences perched comfortably on the bottom rungs of the spiritual life. "Ascend" and "ascend eagerly," John Climacus beseeches in his closing paragraphs. "This is a ladder that we must each climb up for ourselves."

Not, however, *by* ourselves. Despite their emphasis on diligent effort, these are not "self-help" programs but spiritual journeys that, like Jacob's, begin and end with divine grace. As St. Jerome put it in a letter to a widow, "The Christian life is the true Jacob's ladder on which the angels ascend and descend, while the Lord stands above it holding out his hand to those who slip and sustaining by the vision of himself the weary steps of those who ascend."

In a beautiful synthesis of images, Christian writers identified Jacob's ladder with the instrument of our salvation. "Its actual name is the cross of Our Lord Jesus Christ," said St. Zeno of Verona, "since by it he has opened the road of heaven to all who follow him."

Even more, they identified it with the very person of Jesus. A sixth-century Syrian homily compares the cross to a "marvelous ladder" reuniting heaven and earth; it goes on to say that Christ "placed himself on earth like a ladder with many rungs and lifted himself up so that all earthly beings could be raised up by him." St. Bernard and many others agreed: "Christ's earthly life, and especially his Passion, are a real spiritual ladder—the only means by which we will arrive at our destination."

Fanciful? Hardly! Speaking to a young man named Nathanael, Jesus endorsed the image of himself as the ladder of salvation, the vertical "way" of life. In a clear allusion to Genesis 28, he promised Nathanael that he would "see heaven opened and the angels of God ascending and descending upon the Son of Man" (John 1:51).

Wherever we are, then, and with much more reason than Jacob had, we can exclaim that "the Lord is in this place" (Genesis 28:16). Instead of simply throwing us a rescue ladder, he traveled down to make himself Emmanuel, "God with us." As we pick up our cross and follow him, Jesus will help us ascend to our Father.

Who Are You, My Wife?

Questions to Begin

15 minutes
Use a question or two to get warmed up for the reading.

1 What truth is there to the saying "What goes around comes around"?

2 Do you use any herbal medicines or folk remedies? Where did you learn about them?

3 What's a good approach to choosing names for a new baby?
❏ Poll friends and relatives for suggestions.
❏ Pick names that are traditional in your family.
❏ Let your imagination run wild.
❏ Look for ideas in baby-names books.
❏ Select a patron or role model first.
❏ Don't decide until you've met the newborn.

5 minutes
Read the passage aloud. Let individuals take turns reading
paragraphs.

The Reading: Genesis 29:15–30:24

The Unexpected Bride

29:15 Then Laban said to Jacob, "Because you are my kinsman,
should you therefore serve me for nothing? Tell me, what shall your
wages be?" 16 Now Laban had two daughters; the name of the elder
was Leah, and the name of the younger was Rachel. 17 Leah's eyes
were lovely, and Rachel was graceful and beautiful. 18 Jacob loved
Rachel; so he said, "I will serve you seven years for your younger
daughter Rachel." . . . 20 So Jacob served seven years for Rachel, and
they seemed to him but a few days because of the love he had for her.

21 Then Jacob said to Laban, "Give me my wife that I may go
in to her, for my time is completed." 22 So Laban gathered together
all the people of the place, and made a feast. 23 But in the evening
he took his daughter Leah and brought her to Jacob; and he went in
to her. . . . 25 When morning came, it was Leah! And Jacob said to
Laban, "What is this you have done to me? Did I not serve with you
for Rachel? Why then have you deceived me?" 26 Laban said, "This
is not done in our country—giving the younger before the firstborn.
27 Complete the week of this one, and we will give you the other also
in return for serving me another seven years." 28 Jacob did so . . . ;
then Laban gave him his daughter Rachel as a wife. . . . 30 So Jacob
went in to Rachel also, and he loved Rachel more than Leah. He
served Laban for another seven years.

Sisters in Conflict

31 When the LORD saw that Leah was unloved, he opened her womb;
but Rachel was barren. 32 Leah conceived and bore a son, and she
named him Reuben; for she said, "Because the LORD has looked on
my affliction; surely now my husband will love me." 33 She conceived
again and bore a son, and said, "Because the LORD has heard that I
am hated, he has given me this son also"; and she named him Simeon.
34 Again she conceived and bore a son, and said, "Now this time my
husband will be joined to me . . . "; therefore he was named Levi. 35 She
conceived again and bore a son, and said, "This time I will praise the
LORD"; therefore she named him Judah; then she ceased bearing.

30:1 . . . [Rachel] envied her sister; and she said to Jacob, "Give
me children, or I shall die!" 2 Jacob became very angry with Rachel

and said, "Am I in the place of God, who has withheld from you the fruit of the womb?" 3 Then she said, "Here is my maid Bilhah; go in to her, that she may bear upon my knees and that I too may have children through her." . . . 5 And Bilhah conceived and bore Jacob a son. 6 Then Rachel said, "God has judged me, and has also heard my voice and given me a son"; therefore she named him Dan. 7 Rachel's maid Bilhah conceived again and bore Jacob a second son. 8 Then Rachel said, "With mighty wrestlings I have wrestled with my sister, and have prevailed"; so she named him Naphtali. . . .

10 Then Leah's maid Zilpah bore Jacob a son. 11 And Leah said, "Good fortune!" so she named him Gad. 12 Leah's maid Zilpah bore Jacob a second son. 13 And Leah said, "Happy am I! For the women will call me happy"; so she named him Asher.

Husband for Hire

14 . . . Reuben went and found mandrakes in the field, and brought them to his mother Leah. Then Rachel said to Leah, "Please give me some of your son's mandrakes." 15 But she said to her, "Is it a small matter that you have taken away my husband? Would you take away my son's mandrakes also?" Rachel said, "Then he may lie with you tonight for your son's mandrakes." 16 When Jacob came from the field in the evening, Leah went out to meet him, and said, "You must come in to me; for I have hired you with my son's mandrakes." So he lay with her that night. 17 And God heeded Leah, and she conceived and bore Jacob a fifth son. 18 Leah said, "God has given me my hire . . . "; so she named him Issachar. 19 And Leah conceived again, and she bore Jacob a sixth son. 20 Then Leah said, "God has endowed me with a good dowry; now my husband will honor me, because I have borne him six sons"; so she named him Zebulun. 21 Afterwards she bore a daughter, and named her Dinah.

A Mother at Last

22 Then God remembered Rachel, and God heeded her and opened her womb. 23 She conceived and bore a son, and said, "God has taken away my reproach"; 24 and she named him Joseph, saying, "May the Lord add to me another son!"

10 minutes
Choose questions according to your interest and time.

1 Where does the word *serve* (or variations of it) occur in this reading? Compare these instances with the instances of *serve* in 25:23 and 27:29, 37, 40. What do you make of your findings?

2 What similarities can you find between Laban's act of deception and Jacob's (29:21–28; 27:5–29)? How is Jacob like Laban? like Isaac?

3 What do Leah's and Rachel's first quoted statements reveal about them?

4 The side episode involving the mandrakes is curious, to say the least! What does it add to the story?

5 Compare Jacob's reaction to Rachel's childlessness (30:2) with his father's response to Rebekah's (25:21). What does the contrast suggest about Jacob?

6 Does Jacob seem different in chapter 30 from the way he was before? Back up your answers with specific verses.

A Guide to the Reading

If participants have not read this section already, read it aloud. Otherwise go on to "Questions for Application."

29:14–20. Laban oozes concern for Jacob, but his slippery question about wages is motivated by self-concern. After apparently receiving a month's free labor (29:14–15), he wants a formal work agreement. Is it to retain a good shepherd or to ensure that his nephew won't become a moocher? Another possible translation—*"Are* you my kinsman . . . ?"*—suggests that Laban regrets welcoming Jacob as family and wants a laborer-under-contract arrangement that limits his obligations.

Jacob the hard bargainer (25:29–34) has morphed into Jacob the lovesick pushover. Seven years' service is a ridiculously high offer! The original prophecy to Rebekah, confirmed in Isaac's blessings, foresaw brothers and nations serving Jacob (25:23; 27:29, 37, 40). Now, Jacob will serve (30:26, 29; 31:6, 41).

29:21–30. Does Jacob have a sickening sense of déjà vu when, too late, he discovers that "it was Leah!"? A dark tent, one sibling posing as another in borrowed clothing, a sightless victim led astray by his sense of touch—it is a measure-for-measure replay of his own act of trickery (27:18–29). "As Jacob had deceived Isaac with kid dressed as venison," Laurence Turner wryly observes, "so now he is deceived by mutton dressed as lamb." Isaac at least tried to confirm the identity of the son he was about to bless, but Jacob naively assumes that Rachel is the woman under the traditional wedding veil.

More irony. In the Hebrew, Jacob's "Why then have you deceived me?" (29:25) echoes Isaac's description of Jacob's deceit (27:35). Laban's self-righteous defense leaves Jacob speechless because it so deftly evokes his despoiling of Esau.

Laban's little joke gives Jacob a taste of his own medicine, but at Leah and Rachel's expense. The weeklong wedding festivities (29:27) become a humiliating public ordeal for the daughters and set the stage for family conflict.

29:31–30:13. Two sons wrestled for domination in the womb (25:22–26); now two daughters wrestle by means of the womb (30:1, 8). Each wants something the other has. Unloved, unhappy Leah receives God's merciful blessing in the form of six sons and a daughter. Rachel, beloved but barren, turns envious and shrill, demanding from Jacob what only God can give (30:1–2).

Her "Give me children, or I shall die!" evokes Esau, who acted impetuously because he was "about to die" of hunger (25:32). Rachel acts impatiently too. Offering one's maid as a surrogate mother was an acceptable custom (16:1–3), but Rachel's imperious tone suggests more concern about winning than about waiting on God. Indeed, the names Dan and Naphtali (respectively derived from Hebrew words referring to vindication and prevailing in a struggle—30:6, 8) have a competitive edge.

The names Leah gives her sons are more touching than triumphant; they express simple joy at receiving God's favor and poignant longing for Jacob's (29:32, 33, 34, 35).

30:14–21. The dispute over mandrakes, plant roots that were valued as aphrodisiacs and infertility remedies, dramatizes the tensions within Jacob's family. As submissive to his wives as Isaac was to Rebekah, Jacob does as he is told. He sleeps with the maids; he climbs meekly into Leah's bed, which he had apparently abandoned for Rachel's (29:34; 30:15–16). The fruit of this pathetic barter is Issachar, whose name—a wordplay on the idea of hiring for wages—memorializes Jacob's passive servitude (30:18).

Having sons by her maid doesn't satisfy Rachel's desire for children, and mandrakes don't work either. Without their help Leah bears Zebulun and Dinah (30:20–21). The point is that God alone can "open wombs" (29:31; 30:22), and he is unswayed by "magic" roots and manipulation.

30:22–24. God's "remembering" is an active force that reverses hopeless cases (30:22). Just when it seems most unlikely, the gift of fertility comes to Rachel, and the "war of the wombs" climaxes in Joseph's birth.

As Rachel cradles her infant son, we are left pondering the truly unedifying entry into the world of these important, name-giving ancestors of the tribes of Israel. Trickery, envy, dispute—even in these sordid circumstances, God is mysteriously present and graciously works out his purposes. In the fullness of time, he will use even the mess of a marriage between a husband and a wife he doesn't love to bring forth the Savior: through Judah, born to Leah, Jesus will come into the world (29:35; Matthew 1:2–3).

Questions for Application

40 minutes
Choose questions according to your interest and time.

1 People sometimes talk about their mistakes and sins "coming back to haunt" them. Can anything constructive come out of these painful replays?

2 Laban mentions only one reason for switching brides on Jacob (29:26). What other motives might he have had? What effects do hidden agendas have on relationships?

3 What clouds our ability to foresee the negative consequences of our actions? To what degree can a relationship with the Holy Spirit help us overcome this problem?

4 Jacob's first seven years of service for Rachel "seemed to him but a few days because of the love he had for her" (29:20). As you've carried out your own obligations to other people, have you noticed the difference that love makes? What might you do to make love of God and neighbor the driving force behind your everyday activities?

5 Jacob, Rachel, and Leah react differently to their personal problems. How would you describe each character's main challenge at this point? How does each one handle it? In your opinion, who is most successful? What positive and negative lessons can you draw from them for your own life?

6 Most people don't put their faith in mandrakes to obtain what they want, but even religious people sometimes take a superstitious approach to things like medals, statues, and novenas. How can you tell when devotion is deviating into superstition? (See the *Catechism,* section 2111.)

7 When have you realized that God was working in a hidden way through the difficult circumstances in your life?

We use the Scriptures to discover clues about God's hidden presence in our midst.

Steve Mueller, *The Seeker's Guide to Reading the Bible*

Approach to Prayer

15 minutes
Use this approach—or create your own!

♦ God is bigger than we can imagine, even big enough to work out his hidden purposes in situations marred by bad choices and failures. Invite group members to share personal examples of God making "all things work together for good" (Romans 8:28).

Then have someone read out the following prayer, pausing between each sentence so that members can offer their own responses, either silently or out loud. End with a Glory Be.

Eternal Trinity, however much I may come to know you, I humbly acknowledge that I can never fully understand you. Help me to identify and reject any ways of thinking and acting that are really attempts to control you. Forgive me for ever having tried to manipulate you. Right now, I put my whole life into your hands—my ambitions, worries, desires, relationships, problems. Increase my trust, and show me how to work with you.

Saints in the Making

St. Elizabeth of Portugal, Peacemaker

This section is a supplement for individual reading.

St. Elizabeth of Portugal grew to holiness against a dark background of themes familiar to readers of the Jacob story—sibling rivalry, power struggles, loveless marriages, and dysfunctional families. Her personal life was "a great tragedy," says one biographer. That it made her one of history's most determined peacemakers is yet another story of amazing grace.

Born in 1271, Elizabeth grew up in the palace of her grandfather, the king of Aragon, in Spain. He was a profligate who took and tired of three wives and banished his own son.

Elizabeth was married off when she was twelve, a pawn in the complex world of European politics. Her husband, King Denis of Portugal, viewed the marriage only as a way to strengthen his claim to the throne. Unloved, Elizabeth watched as Denis took up with one woman after another. She felt the sting of jealousy, says her first biographer, yet cultivated "peace of heart" and conquered bitterness. This inner peace was surely tested when Denis had the effrontery to make Elizabeth the guardian of his illegitimate children.

In 1291, Elizabeth resolved a quarrel between her husband and his brother. Civil war was averted, and Elizabeth became popularly known as the Peacemaker. Similar successes followed. But the hostility between Denis and their son, Alfonso, posed the greatest challenge to Elizabeth's peacekeeping skills. Because Denis favored an illegitimate son, Alfonso made a failed attempt to kill his half brother and take his father's throne. Elizabeth was falsely accused of encouraging the plot and was banished from Denis's court. "What a life of bitterness I am leading!" she wrote her brother during that period. "On whom but God can I lean?"

Eventually restored as queen, Elizabeth obtained a full pardon for Alfonso; however, in 1320, he organized another futile assassination attempt. Again, Elizabeth effected a reconciliation. By 1323, though, Alfonso was marching on Lisbon with a substantial army, intent on wresting the throne from his father. This time, Elizabeth rode on a mule right out onto the battlefield to make her plea for peace. Her heroism and holiness won the day.

It wasn't for nothing that Pope Urban VIII named this valiant woman the patroness of peace!

Between Discussions

You Reap What You Sow

Most of us know what it's like to feel trapped in a bad situation of our own making—a job, a relationship, a habit. We can empathize with Jacob and imagine some of the "if only's" running through his mind as he endures hard days of outdoor labor and hard nights of dissension in the family tents. *If only I hadn't deceived my father and brother. If only I'd waited patiently for the blessing to come to me . . .*

Jacob's cleverness has gotten him nowhere. After fourteen years with Laban, what does he have? Eleven children and swelling herds of livestock are evidence that God's blessing of life and fertility rests on him in a special way. But like a popular star whose agent and accountant help themselves to most of the profits, Jacob is not reaping the benefits. The problem is his position as a younger relative in the household of his uncle Laban, who ultimately retains control of everything that Jacob has worked for. Not quite a slave but not quite free, Jacob is still fundamentally an exile, with no home, family, or possessions to call his own.

Jacob the deceiver, who treated God and his father with contempt (27:20), has met his match in his wily uncle. His story invites us to reflect on a sobering spiritual principle: "Do not be deceived; God is not mocked, for you reap whatever you sow" (Galatians 6:7).

Joseph's birth signals a change in Jacob's fortunes and an end to his passivity. In the passages skipped in our weekly readings (30:25–43), Jacob completes his work contract and presents Laban with a request to take his family home to Canaan (30:25–26). He is not working from a position of strength, however. His own words underline his dependence as a servant on his uncle-master (in the Hebrew of 30:26, he uses forms of the word *serve* three times when speaking of himself). And his references to "my" wives and "my" children are a bit of bravado: correctly, he suspects that greedy Laban will contest his claim, on the basis of customary laws governing property and family life (31:43).

Laban knows full well that he owes his prosperity to Jacob, but he deflects the request by treating it as the opener to another negotiating session over the price of Jacob's future services (30:27–28, 31). Will Jacob handle this more shrewdly than he did his negotiations for Rachel (29:18, 27)? Initially, it appears not. He drops his request and consents to keep on serving Laban in return for all the abnormally colored sheep and goats to be born in his herds. Since the proposal seems guaranteed to shortchange Jacob, it gets Laban's enthusiastic endorsement. He takes immediate steps to reduce whatever minuscule gain Jacob can expect (30:31–36).

But the laugh is on Laban. Over the next six years, Jacob manipulates the breeding of the livestock to his own advantage by an obscure process of prenatal conditioning through visual aids (30:37–42). You might well raise a quizzical eyebrow at the folkloric idea that having sheep and goats look at peeled, streaky sticks can result in the birth of "speckled and spotted" lambs and kids. The main point, though, is that God makes this strategy fruitful. Jacob's success comes fundamentally not by magic, accident, skill, or cleverness. As he tells Rachel and Leah, "God has taken away the livestock of your father, and given them to me" (31:9). (Are we as clear about the source of whatever prosperity and blessing we ourselves experience?)

Jacob has taken hold of the blessing through hard work and self-discipline. But the blessing is a free and undeserved expression of God's merciful kindness, and Jacob knows it. Like the increase in his family, which came about when God "looked on" Leah in her affliction (29:32) and "remembered Rachel" in her distress (30:22), the increase in Jacob's flocks comes about because God looks with compassion on his suffering: "I have seen all that Laban is doing to you" (31:12).

As things turn out, it is Laban who is left mulling over "if only's": *If only I'd been content with the increase I had already received through Jacob.* By trying to contain Jacob's blessing so that he alone could profit from it, Laban, too, treated God with contempt. In the end, he is beaten at his own game, stuck with a dwindling flock of feeble animals while Jacob grows "exceedingly rich," owning "large flocks" and everything their proceeds can buy—"male and female slaves, and camels and donkeys" (30:42–43).

Laban's story stands as a cautionary tale illustrating not only "you reap what you sow" but also "the measure you give will be the measure you get" (Matthew 7:2).

Escape into Danger

Questions to Begin

15 minutes
Use a question or two to get warmed up for the reading.

1 How do you react to chase scenes and dramatic escapes in books and movies? Which ones have especially impressed you—or can you tell such a story from your own life?

2 Describe an incident in which you or someone in your family lost something and then found it in an unlikely place.

3 What's the most lavish gift you've ever received? What's the most lavish gift you've ever given?

5 minutes
Read the passage aloud. Let individuals take turns reading
paragraphs.

The Reading: Genesis 31:1–7, 14–55; 32:1–20

Family Consultation

31:1 Now Jacob heard that the sons of Laban were saying, "Jacob has taken all that was our father's; he has gained all this wealth from what belonged to our father." 2 And Jacob saw that Laban did not regard him as favorably as he did before. 3 Then the LORD said to Jacob, "Return to the land of your ancestors and to your kindred, and I will be with you." 4 So Jacob sent and called Rachel and Leah into the field where his flock was, 5 and said to them, "I see that your father does not regard me as favorably as he did before. But the God of my father has been with me. 6 You know that I have served your father with all my strength; 7 yet your father has cheated me and changed my wages ten times, but God did not permit him to harm me. . . . "

14 Then Rachel and Leah answered him, "Is there any portion or inheritance left to us in our father's house? 15 Are we not regarded by him as foreigners? For he has sold us, and he has been using up the money given for us. 16 All the property that God has taken away from our father belongs to us and to our children; now then, do whatever God has said to you."

Still Running, after All These Years

17 So Jacob arose, and set his children and his wives on camels; 18 and he drove away all his livestock, all the property that he had gained, the livestock in his possession that he had acquired in Paddan-aram, to go to his father Isaac in the land of Canaan.

19 Now Laban had gone to shear his sheep, and Rachel stole her father's household gods. 20 And Jacob deceived Laban the Aramean, in that he did not tell him that he intended to flee. 21 So he fled with all that he had; starting out he crossed the Euphrates, and set his face toward the hill country of Gilead.

22 On the third day Laban was told that Jacob had fled. 23 So he took his kinsfolk with him and pursued him for seven days until he caught up with him in the hill country of Gilead. 24 But God came to Laban the Aramean in a dream by night, and said to him, "Take heed that you say not a word to Jacob, either good or bad." . . .

Showdown!

26 Laban said to Jacob, "What have you done? You have deceived me, and carried away my daughters like captives of the sword. 27 Why did you flee secretly and deceive me and not tell me? I would have sent you away with mirth and songs, with tambourine and lyre. 28 And why did you not permit me to kiss my sons and my daughters farewell? What you have done is foolish. 29 It is in my power to do you harm; but the God of your father spoke to me last night, saying, 'Take heed that you speak to Jacob neither good nor bad.' 30 Even though you had to go because you longed greatly for your father's house, why did you steal my gods?" 31 Jacob answered Laban, "Because I was afraid, for I thought that you would take your daughters from me by force. 32 But anyone with whom you find your gods shall not live. In the presence of our kinsfolk, point out what I have that is yours, and take it." Now Jacob did not know that Rachel had stolen the gods.

Rachel's Revenge

33 So Laban went into Jacob's tent, and into Leah's tent, and into the tent of the two maids, but he did not find them. And he went out of Leah's tent, and entered Rachel's. 34 Now Rachel had taken the household gods and put them in the camel's saddle, and sat on them. Laban felt all about in the tent, but did not find them. 35 And she said to her father, "Let not my lord be angry that I cannot rise before you, for the way of women is upon me." So he searched, but did not find the household gods.

Laban Loses Face

36 Then Jacob became angry, and upbraided Laban. Jacob said to Laban, "What is my offense? What is my sin, that you have hotly pursued me? 37 Although you have felt about through all my goods, what have you found of all your household goods? Set it here before my kinsfolk and your kinsfolk, so that they may decide between us two. 38 These twenty years I have been with you; your ewes and your female goats have not miscarried, and I have not eaten the rams of your flocks. 39 That which was torn by wild beasts I did not bring to you; I bore the loss of it myself; of my hand you required it, whether stolen by day or stolen by night. 40 It was like this with me: by day the heat consumed me, and the cold by night, and my sleep fled from my eyes.

41 These twenty years I have been in your house; I served you fourteen years for your two daughters, and six years for your flock, and you have changed my wages ten times. 42 If the God of my father, the God of Abraham and the Fear of Isaac, had not been on my side, surely now you would have sent me away empty-handed. God saw my affliction and the labor of my hands, and rebuked you last night."

A Nonaggression Treaty

43 Then Laban answered and said to Jacob, "The daughters are my daughters, the children are my children, the flocks are my flocks, and all that you see is mine. But what can I do today about these daughters of mine, or about their children whom they have borne? 44 Come now, let us make a covenant, you and I; and let it be a witness between you and me." 45 So Jacob took a stone, and set it up as a pillar. 46 And Jacob said to his kinsfolk, "Gather stones," and they took stones, and made a heap; and they ate there by the heap. . . . 48 Laban said, "This heap is a witness between you and me today." . . . 50 If you ill-treat my daughters, or if you take wives in addition to my daughters, though no one else is with us, remember that God is witness between you and me."

51 Then Laban said to Jacob, "See this heap and see the pillar, which I have set between you and me. 52 This heap is a witness, and the pillar is a witness, that I will not pass beyond this heap to you, and you will not pass beyond this heap and this pillar to me, for harm. 53 May the God of Abraham and the God of Nahor"—the God of their father—"judge between us." So Jacob swore by the Fear of his father Isaac, 54 and Jacob offered a sacrifice on the height and called his kinsfolk to eat bread; and they ate bread and tarried all night in the hill country.

55 Early in the morning Laban rose up, and kissed his grandchildren and his daughters and blessed them; then he departed and returned home.

Homeward Bound

32:1 Jacob went on his way and the angels of God met him. . . .

3 Jacob sent messengers before him to his brother Esau in the land of Seir, the country of Edom, 4 instructing them, "Thus you shall say to my lord Esau: Thus says your servant Jacob, 'I have lived with

Laban as an alien, and stayed until now; 5 and I have oxen, donkeys, flocks, male and female slaves; and I have sent to tell my lord, in order that I may find favor in your sight.'"

6 The messengers returned to Jacob, saying, "We came to your brother Esau, and he is coming to meet you, and four hundred men are with him." 7 Then Jacob was greatly afraid and distressed; and he divided the people that were with him, and the flocks and herds and camels, into two companies, 8 thinking, "If Esau comes to the one company and destroys it, then the company that is left will escape."

9 And Jacob said, "O God of my father Abraham and God of my father Isaac, O LORD who said to me, 'Return to your country and to your kindred, and I will do you good,' 10 I am not worthy of the least of all the steadfast love and all the faithfulness that you have shown to your servant, for with only my staff I crossed this Jordan; and now I have become two companies. 11 Deliver me, please, from the hand of my brother, from the hand of Esau, for I am afraid of him; he may come and kill us all, the mothers with the children. 12 Yet you have said, 'I will surely do you good, and make your offspring as the sand of the sea, which cannot be counted because of their number.'"

A Peace Offering for Esau

13 So he spent that night there, and from what he had with him he took a present for his brother Esau, 14 two hundred female goats and twenty male goats, two hundred ewes and twenty rams, 15 thirty milch camels and their colts, forty cows and ten bulls, twenty female donkeys and ten male donkeys. 16 These he delivered into the hand of his servants, every drove by itself, and said to his servants, "Pass on ahead of me, and put a space between drove and drove." 17 He instructed the foremost, "When Esau my brother meets you, and asks you, 'To whom do you belong? Where are you going? And whose are these ahead of you?' 18 then you shall say, 'They belong to your servant Jacob; they are a present sent to my lord Esau; and moreover he is behind us.'" 19 He likewise instructed the second and the third and all who followed the droves, "You shall say the same thing to Esau when you meet him, 20 and you shall say, 'Moreover your servant Jacob is behind us.'" For he thought, "I may appease him with the present that goes ahead of me, and afterwards I shall see his face; perhaps he will accept me."

10 minutes
Choose questions according to your interest and time.

1　What assurance does Jacob have that it is safe to return home? Why do Rachel and Leah agree to go along? Is a secret escape necessary?

2　Notice how Jacob refers to God in speaking to his wives (31:5) and how he speaks to God in prayer (32:9–12). What do his words suggest about his developing relationship with God?

3　Compare 31:24 with 31:26–30. Does Laban disobey God's command?

4　Compare 31:33–35 with 27:18–27 and 29:21–25. In the scene from this week's reading, what echoes of the first two scenes of "deception in a tent" can you find? What is different?

5　Based on the incidents in this week's reading, choose three adjectives that describe Laban. Give specific verses to back up your choices.

6　Locate the verses where Jacob acknowledges that his blessings come from God. Is he sincere, or is this a replay of 27:20?

A Guide to the Reading

If participants have not read this section already, read it aloud. Otherwise go on to "Questions for Application."

31:1–16. Laban's family is split into two camps. On one side are his sons, whose mutterings about Jacob's prosperity parallel their father's menacing looks (31:1–2). On the other are Laban's daughters, who emphatically declare themselves for Jacob.

Naturally, Jacob presents his case persuasively. In an outdoor consultation held away from prying ears, he stresses his integrity, Laban's trickery, and his experience of God's blessing (31:5–13). Rachel and Leah need no urging. Laban has used them as bargaining chips to increase his fortunes. Contrary to custom, they will never inherit any of the bride price that Jacob paid in the form of sweat equity (31:14–15; 29:18, 27). Feeling disrespected, the sisters join in a rare show of solidarity. In formal, legal terms, they repudiate their tie to Laban and lay claim to their rightful share of his wealth (31:14–16).

31:17–32. Sheepshearing was a springtime activity that took place in far-off pastures. With Laban and his menfolk preoccupied, it is the perfect time to flee (31:19). But why is Jacob still playing the fugitive when he has a divine mandate to return home? Assured again of God's protection (31:3), why does he fear Laban (31:31)? Jacob's continued references to "the God of my father" (31:5, 42)—and not "my God" (28:21)—suggest that his trust remains somewhat provisional.

We might wonder about Rachel's motivation for stealing some small figurines, Laban's "household gods" (31:19). Such idols were associated with a family's prosperity and protection and could signify legal title to an inheritance. Sometimes they were used for divination. Perhaps Rachel takes the gods to prevent Laban from detecting her family's escape. Perhaps she wants to ensure possession of the goods and livestock that Jacob is taking. Or is the theft primarily an act of spite?

Laban follows up his seven-day pursuit with an emotional performance that highlights his hypocrisy (31:26–28). Given his record, his tone of injured innocence and fatherly affection is unconvincing. Leah and Rachel must be rolling their eyes as they listen! But when Jacob vows death to any thief of Laban's goods (31:32), the comic scene threatens to turn tragic.

31:33–35. No, this is a comedy after all, with Laban
playing the buffoon as he rummages ineffectually through the tents.
Self-possessed Rachel outmaneuvers her father—sweet revenge
for his having made a joke of her wedding night! Sitting on his idols
implies contempt, especially if Rachel really is having her period
(in many ancient societies, a menstruating woman was considered
ritually impure: see Leviticus 15:19–24).

31:36–42. Jacob uses judicial language to charge Laban
with thievery and call onlookers to render a verdict (31:36–37). His
evidence, a summary of Laban's two-decade exploitation of his loyal
service, is compelling. Especially damning is Jacob's accusation
that Laban intended to deny him all his wages (31:38–42).

Significantly, Jacob attributes his vindication and survival
not to his own labor or cleverness but to God's intervention on
behalf of the weak. The unusual title "Fear of Isaac" evokes God's
protection and majesty and may allude to Laban's warning dream
(31:29, 42, 53).

31:43–55. Exposed as a cheat, Laban saves face with
a hollow show of magnanimity—a "let bygones be bygones" and a
truce proposal (31:43–44). Stone memorials and a ceremonial meal
seal the agreement, which is not a warm reconciliation but a coolly
negotiated nonaggression pact. Notice that there is no farewell
embrace for Jacob (compare with 29:13).

32:3–20. No longer on guard about what lies behind,
Jacob is on edge about what lies ahead. Is Esau still breathing
murder? The reappearance of angels at the border bodes well (32:1;
28:12), but news that Esau is advancing with what sounds like a
troop of soldiers is disturbing (32:6). In a rare commentary on a
biblical character's psychological state, we are told that Jacob is
scared witless (32:7).

Jacob's prayer (32:9–12) is a genuine cry for help. But does
it reflect some inner purification, or is it just one of several tactics
Jacob uses in handling the crisis shrewdly? These tactics include
a calculatedly servile message that hints at a possible payoff to
Esau (32:4–5), a plan for damage control (32:7–8), and lavish gifts
spaced for maximum effect (32:13–20).

Jacob bought Esau's birthright with one bowl of stew. Can
an offering of 550 animals buy him Esau's favor?

Questions for Application

40 minutes
Choose questions according to your interest and time.

1 Even though Laban tricked and cheated him, Jacob apparently gave him top-notch service as a shepherd and herdsman. What is the lesson for us?

2 Jacob believed that God was with him during his time of servitude. From your own experience and observation, how does a sense of God's presence affect a person's experience of trial?

3 Read the discussion of God's discipline in Hebrews 12:5–11. Do you think it applies to Jacob's experience? What about your own?

4 Laban's dream gives him his own personal encounter with God. Why isn't he changed by it?

5 Do you think Laban really believes his self-righteous description of himself as the injured party who is reasonable and magnanimous? Is it possible to have such distorted perceptions of oneself? How can a person acquire self-knowledge?

6 When you are afraid, do you naturally turn to God? What could you do to grow in your ability to entrust worries, large and small, to the Lord?

The group should never close off its search for the Bible's beauty, meaning, and goodness. . . . Wonder should move the group to ponder, to weigh what it senses and learns as it continues to explore.

Eugene LeVerdiere, S.S.S., "Bible Study: Sowing the Seed," *Church*

Approach to Prayer

15 minutes
Use this approach—or create your own!

♦ Jacob's prayer in terror is a model for us, encouraging us to bring our own fears to God. Invite participants to mention some of their fears and worries. Then, intercede for one another by taking turns praying aloud for each participant's intention, following each prayer with a group response, such as "Lord, hear our prayer."

End with an Our Father or with the following prayer, inspired by Jacob's.

O God our Father, you are
    merciful. Your word is
    true.
We do not deserve the steadfast
    love and faithfulness that
    you have shown us.
When we were far from you
    and had nothing, you
    blessed us with the gift of
    your Son, your life, and
    the promise of an eternal
    inheritance.
Deliver us from our fears and
    from every evil.
Protect and keep us and those
    we love.
We praise and thank you
    for your love and your
    promises.
Amen.

A Living Tradition

Devil Ain't Got Nothin' on Me

This section is a supplement for individual reading.

St. Caesarius of Arles (470–543) was the foremost bishop of Gaul (modern-day France) during a period made difficult by barbarian invasions. A skilled administrator and theologian, he was especially appreciated as a preacher—and no wonder. He kept his sermons short—fifteen minutes or under—and clear, with ordinary-life illustrations that peasants and townspeople could relate to. When he spoke on Old Testament subjects, as in this sermon about Jacob's flight from Laban, St. Caesarius favored allegorical interpretations that looked ahead to Christ and made connections with the gospel.

As Jacob was returning to his own country, Laban and his companions pursued them. Upon examination of Jacob's substance Laban found nothing of his, and, therefore, he could not hold him. Laban here is not unfittingly said to stand as a figure of the devil, because he both served idols and was opposed to blessed Jacob who prefigured the Lord. For this reason he pursued Jacob but was unable to find anything of his own with him. Listen to the true Jacob declaring this fact in the Gospel: "Behold the prince of the world is coming, and in me he will find nothing" [John 14:30].

May the divine mercy grant that our adversary may find nothing of his works in us, for if he finds nothing of his own, he will not be able to keep us or recall us from eternal life.

Therefore, dearly beloved, let us look at the treasury of our conscience, let us examine the secret places of our heart, and if we find nothing there which belongs to the devil let us rejoice and thank God. With his help let us strive as well as we can that the doors of our heart may always be open for Christ but closed forever to the devil. However, if we recognize something of the devil's works or cunning in our souls, let us hasten to cast it out and get rid of it as deadly poison. Then when the devil wants to ensnare us and can find nothing which belongs to him, he will depart in confusion, while we can thank God with the prophet and shout to the Lord: "You have saved us from our foes, and have put to confusion those who hate us" [Psalm 44:7].

Between Discussions

Hero with an Off-White Hat

The confrontation between Jacob and Laban reads like a classic "good guy–bad guy" showdown. Of course, Laban wears the black hat. But is Jacob worthy of the white one?

Just a couple of chapters ago, he was a passive, pathetic figure who didn't even wear the pants in the family, let alone a halo. Before that, he was a coldly deliberate exploiter and deceiver of his own father and brother. Has Jacob really been changed by grace, or is the old self-interested opportunist waiting in the wings? We wonder. And so, as the story pauses between Laban's exit and Esau's reentrance, we may want to reflect on some issues it raises for us—the consequences of sin, the effects of grace, and the limits of personal change.

First, a look at Laban, who serves as Jacob's antithesis. He is the wily manipulator whose shady character is apparent long before Jacob appears. Earlier, in his biblical debut (24), Laban welcomed Abraham's servant, who had traveled from afar in search of a suitable wife for Isaac. The servant had met Rebekah (seemingly at the very well where Jacob later meets Rachel) and had given her some expensive jewelry. Laban rushed to greet the traveler "as soon as he had seen the nose-ring, and the bracelets on his sister's arms" (24:30)—strongly suggesting hospitality driven by greed. Medieval Jewish sages proposed that Laban greeted Jacob so warmly because he remembered Isaac's servant and his ten gift-bearing camels (24:10) and embraced Jacob only to determine whether he was wearing a money belt filled with gold!

Laban remains in character from start to finish. He prospers because of Jacob's blessing and even recognizes that "the Lord" is responsible (30:27). He encounters the Lord in a warning dream (31:24, 29) and understands that this God is sovereign, nothing like the idols he has been relying on. But is Laban awed and grateful? Does he repent of acting unjustly? No, like the rich and greedy farmer in Jesus' parable (Luke 12:16–21), he is forever a "me first" hoarder and, ultimately, a loser. By refusing every opportunity to rethink his approach to life, Laban loses everything he schemed to obtain.

Where Laban is a flat character, Jacob is complex. His early actions mark him as a kindred spirit of his devious kinsman.

But in the night dream at Bethel, grace breaks in, and Jacob recognizes it (28:17). In fact, his awed reaction is "unprecedented in the patriarchal stories," says Nahum Sarna. "Neither Abraham nor Isaac exhibit any surprise at their initial experience of God's sudden self-revelation" (12:1; 26:2).

Running into God knocks Jacob off balance and onto a new road. Twenty years later, he still appears to be mulling over the mystery of God's merciful attention to a man with a guilty conscience: "I am not worthy of the least of all the steadfast love and all the faithfulness that you have shown to your servant" (32:10).

But not even the contrite escape sin's inescapable consequences. Having connived to obtain God's blessing, Jacob pays the high price of twenty years of hard labor for Laban. Does it change him? The picture is mixed.

Jacob's prayer for help (32:9–12) seems genuinely humble, but the fact that it is inspired by fear and followed by shrewd planning leaves room for questions. His humility "would carry greater conviction," Laurence Turner observes, "if it were allied to penitence." Jacob never does apologize for his past behavior, though the gifts he sends Esau may perhaps be read as a confession of guilt and an attempt at restitution. And while he seeks a reconciliation that will ensure his survival, Jacob expresses no desire for a warm brotherly relationship.

In some ways, Jacob reminds me of certain saints who had to wage lifelong battles against some negative personal tendency like irritability, depression, or anxiety. He is "a fascinating study in the differences that God does, and does not, make in a recalcitrant and willful personality," says Old Testament scholar R. W. L. Moberly. Even after another transforming encounter with God (discussed in week 6), Jacob remains flawed.

Somehow, I find encouragement in the thought of flawed Jacob, limping along toward the God who calls and blesses. He injects realism into my strivings for the perfection Jesus calls us to; he stands as a caution about the possibility of total personality makeovers—whether for my children, my spouse, or myself. I find Jacob most instructive precisely because he wears an off-white hat.

FACE TO FACE AT LAST

Questions to Begin

15 minutes
Use a question or two to get warmed up for the reading.

---

1 What high school sports did you engage in?
❏ basketball
❏ football
❏ soccer
❏ swimming
❏ tennis
❏ track
❏ volleyball
❏ wrestling
❏ other
❏ none

---

2 Describe a situation in which you dreaded having to meet or talk with someone.

5 minutes
Read the passage aloud. Let individuals take turns reading paragraphs.

The Reading: Genesis 32:22–33:17

Struggle and Blessing

32:22 The same night he got up and took his two wives, his two maids, and his eleven children, and crossed the ford of the Jabbok. 23 He took them and sent them across the stream, and likewise everything that he had. 24 Jacob was left alone; and a man wrestled with him until daybreak. 25 When the mana saw that he did not prevail against Jacob, he struck him on the hip socket; and Jacob's hip was put out of joint as he wrestled with him. 26 Then he said, "Let me go, for the day is breaking." But Jacob said, "I will not let you go, unless you bless me." 27 So he said to him, "What is your name?" And he said, "Jacob." 28 Then the mana said, "You shall no longer be called Jacob, but Israel,b for you have striven with God and with humans,c and have prevailed." 29 Then Jacob asked him, "Please tell me your name." But he said, "Why is it that you ask my name?" And there he blessed him. 30 So Jacob called the place Peniel,d saying, "For I have seen God face to face, and yet my life is preserved." 31 The sun rose upon him as he passed Penuel, limping because of his hip. . . .

The Brothers Meet

33:1 Now Jacob looked up and saw Esau coming, and four hundred men with him. So he divided the children among Leah and Rachel and the two maids. 2 He put the maids with their children in front, then Leah with her children, and Rachel and Joseph last of all. 3 He himself went on ahead of them, bowing himself to the ground seven times, until he came near his brother.

4 But Esau ran to meet him, and embraced him, and fell on his neck and kissed him, and they wept. 5 When Esau looked up and saw the women and children, he said, "Who are these with you?" Jacob said, "The children whom God has graciously given your servant." 6 Then the maids drew near, they and their children, and bowed down;

---

a Hebrew *he*
b That is "The one who strives with God" or "God strives."
c Or with divine and human beings
d That is "The face of God."

7 Leah likewise and her children drew near and bowed down; and finally Joseph and Rachel drew near, and they bowed down. 8 Esau said, "What do you mean by all this company that I met?" Jacob answered, "To find favor with my lord." 9 But Esau said, "I have enough, my brother; keep what you have for yourself." 10 Jacob said, "No, please; if I find favor with you, then accept my present from my hand; for truly to see your face is like seeing the face of God—since you have received me with such favor. 11 Please accept my gift that is brought to you, because God has dealt graciously with me, and because I have everything I want." So he urged him, and he took it.

12 Then Esau said, "Let us journey on our way, and I will go alongside you." 13 But Jacob said to him, "My lord knows that the children are frail and that the flocks and herds, which are nursing, are a care to me; and if they are overdriven for one day, all the flocks will die. 14 Let my lord pass on ahead of his servant, and I will lead on slowly, according to the pace of the cattle that are before me and according to the pace of the children, until I come to my lord in Seir."

15 So Esau said, "Let me leave with you some of the people who are with me." But he said, "Why should my lord be so kind to me?" 16 So Esau returned that day on his way to Seir. 17 But Jacob journeyed to Succoth,e and built himself a house, and made booths for his cattle; therefore the place is called Succoth.

e That is "Booths."

10 minutes
Choose questions according to your interest and time.

1 What might be the significance of Jacob's limping after his nighttime encounter?

2 Compare Jacob's way of addressing Esau with Esau's way of addressing Jacob. What does the difference indicate about their relationship?

3 Esau weeps (33:4). When was the last time we saw him weeping? How do the two scenes of his weeping compare with each other? How has Esau changed? How has he not changed?

4 Considering his earlier hatred of Jacob (27:41), why does Esau welcome Jacob when he returns?

5 Compare Jacob's statements in 32:30 and 33:10 about seeing God's face. What connection is there between the two incidents? What is the connection between seeing God's face and seeing a human face?

6 What portrait of Esau emerges from the readings in weeks 1, 2, and 6?

A Guide to the Reading

If participants have not read this section already, read it aloud.
Otherwise go on to "Questions for Application."

32:22–23. The Jabbok River flows swiftly between steep hills. In the springtime, it runs high after the rains. Getting a group of adults, children, and livestock across the stream at night would be a dangerous undertaking. Apparently Jacob feels a sense of urgency. Perhaps he wants to make sure that he meets Esau before the pacifying effect of his gifts wears off.

32:24–31. Jacob's return is marked by a strange nighttime encounter. Who is the "man" who attacks him in the darkness? Surely he is not human. Neither, as some have argued, is he a river demon trying to prevent Jacob from crossing the stream, for Jacob has already crossed it (32:22–23). Neither is he God, for God is not afraid of the dawn (32:26). Yet in some mysterious way, the wrestling *is* an encounter with God (32:30).

Various interpretations have been offered for this obscure incident. Perhaps the wrestling is a subconscious reflection of Jacob's relationship with his brother, with whom he has been wrestling from the womb (25:22, 26). Perhaps the incident symbolizes the process of change that Jacob has undergone. After stealing his brother's blessing, Jacob did achieve success; but he has gotten his blessings by hard work, even by suffering, not as an automatic gift. Jacob the deceiver has felt the pain of being deceived. Thus the nocturnal wrestling match that leads to a blessing may symbolize the course of Jacob's life: he has received a blessing for which he has struggled, replacing the blessing that he stole.

In Hebrew, the original meaning of Jacob's new name, Israel (32:28), may have been "He who is upright with God." Thus the change of name may symbolize his transformation from crookedness to integrity—a transformation that has been in process for twenty years. In various ways, then, the nighttime encounter may reflect the fact that Jacob has overcome his past. Ready to walk boldly into the future, he goes forth to meet the dawn (32:31)—and his brother.

33:1–17. Jacob used to view Esau as a boorish dullard who could easily be outsmarted and whose feelings could be totally disregarded. No longer! Jacob now approaches Esau like a disobedient vassal coming contritely into the presence of his king. Jacob's ceremonial presentation of his wives and children and his sevenfold bowing signify his total submission to his brother. Isaac's blessing of Jacob had made him supreme over his kin: "Be lord over your brothers, and may your mother's sons bow down to you" (27:29). A repentant Jacob now enacts his relinquishment of this stolen blessing.

Esau greets Jacob affectionately (33:4), like the father greeting the prodigal son (compare with Luke 15:20). With a kiss signifying forgiveness, Esau erases the deceptive kiss by which Jacob shattered the family (27:26).

Jacob speaks to Esau of his experience of God's kindness: God "has graciously given," Jacob tells Esau (33:5). The Hebrew word has the sense of both generosity and mercy. Jacob could have said, "God has blessed me." But that might have sounded like Jacob was declaring that his wives, children, and flocks represented the stolen blessing. By his choice of words, Jacob acknowledges that his prosperity is not a result of his dishonesty and cleverness but is an expression of God's kindness. If in any sense Jacob has benefited from his father's blessing, the blessings have come to him in the form of God's mercy to a sinner—and through Jacob's hard work.

Esau has done well (33:9). Perhaps Isaac's idea of the paternal blessing (27:33–37) was inadequate. Even though Jacob received the blessing, that did *not* mean there was nothing left for Esau. Esau too has experienced his father's blessing. God has not been limited by human ideas of how he must act.

Despite Esau's prosperity, Jacob urges him to "accept my gift" (33:11). Jacob says literally "my blessing"—the very word used in 27:35–36. In this way, Jacob implies that his gift is reparation for the blessing that he stole. Esau's acceptance signals his forgiveness of Jacob.

Esau assumes that Jacob plans to join him in Seir (33:12). But Jacob puts him off. "Until I come to my lord in Seir" (33:14) is a polite way of declining to accompany his brother without refusing him to his face. Jacob has come to respect his brother, but it is a respect born of fear. Jacob suspects that Esau harbors resentment. It is no longer possible for the brothers to achieve an intimate brotherly relationship. But did they ever have one?

Questions for Application

40 minutes
Choose questions according to your interest and time.

1 Have you ever felt as if you were wrestling with God? What effect has this experience had on you?

2 What are the ingredients for true reconciliation between people when a serious wrong has been committed?

3 How important are words in expressing repentance and seeking forgiveness? How important are actions?

4 What role does the passage of time play in overcoming injury and conflict between people?

5 Can a broken personal relationship ever be fully repaired?

6 How can trust be reestablished with a person after they have been guilty of betrayal or deception?

7 Is distance sometimes better than nearness for maintaining some personal relationships?

8 Does reconciliation between people necessarily lead to intimacy and friendship between them?

9 For personal reflection: With whom do you need to be reconciled? What is holding you back? How could you find God's help to proceed? What step should you take?

It helps us every once in a while to admit that we simply do not know what a particular biblical passage means or that we see only a small part of the meaning.

James A. Fischer, *How to Read the Bible*

Approach to Prayer

15 minutes
Use this approach—or create your own!

♦ Place before God any source of difficulty or pain with which you are struggling.

Let one person read aloud this statement of St. Francis de Sales: "God never wrestles with us except in order to give himself to us and to bless us."

Take a few minutes for silent prayer. Then allow a few minutes for anyone to mention some area of life in which they are struggling to know God's will or understand his ways or trust him more.

Pray an Our Father together.

End by having a participant read aloud St. Francis de Sales's statement again as a final blessing, concluding with the words "Let us go in peace."

Saints in the Making

Wrestling with God

This section is a supplement for individual reading.

In April 1995, six-year-old John-Paul Floyd, the son of Gregory and Maureen Floyd, was struck and killed by a car in front of their New Jersey home. In *A Grief Unveiled,* published four years later, Gregory chronicled the couple's anguish in the aftermath of their son's death. Jacob's wrestling, he wrote, seemed a fitting image for his own experience.

All the philosophy and theology in the world could not touch my pain. Yet even in my pain I still had to wrestle with the awful question: Why?

Wrestling is a good biblical sport. Jacob wrestled with the angel at Peniel and would not let him go until he received the blessing he sought. . . . This is a remarkable passage. Jacob receives a blessing because he fought! . . . Job wrestled with his "friends" and with God himself . . . Jesus wrestled with his Father's will in Gethsemane. . . . In these incidents and in many others, the dynamic is wrestle and surrender. The wrestling is between God and humanity, and it is as old as death. But it does not appear to be a sign of rebellion or pride. God created the mind that questions and the heart that feels, and thus the need to understand. . . . And so I had to wrestle with God, if only to come to the point of realizing that there are some things I may never understand. God is unafraid of the wrestling. He is always waiting, ready to engage. . . .

I reached the point where I could only surrender to the mystery of God's will. . . . At a certain point, a moment of grace, God's will ceases to be a problem and becomes a mystery. I admit that I do not know about these things. I know that I will not answer this question and that is my act of faith: to believe with the unanswered question. I must accept that God allows things to happen that he did not design, or accept that his designs, which initially transcend my capacity to understand, rest preeminent and secure and are never ultimately thwarted by evil. . . .

I do not know what he is doing through Johnny's death. I do not understand why it happened. I do not know how God is working it to the good, as he promises he will (Romans 8:28). . . . I hope that God will permit us not to waste this suffering. I hope that suffering embraced might become true compassion.

After Words

At the end of our readings, Jacob is still many miles from home, and, strangely, he seems in no hurry to complete his return to his father. After parting from Esau, Jacob stays in nearby Succoth for a while—long enough to build a house (33:17). Then he crosses the Jordan River into what is now the Palestinian territories, where he settles at Shechem. Here Jacob shows no sign of intending to complete his journey home, for he buys land in Shechem, a sign of putting down roots (33:19). A local man, however, rapes and abducts his daughter, Dinah, and his sons free her at the cost of much bloodshed, making peaceful relations with the neighbors impossible (chapter 34; see page 88). Forced to move on, Jacob travels south through Bethel, where God first appeared to him. Farther on, Rachel gives birth to a son and dies in childbirth. As she endures her hard labor, she is consoled by the knowledge that God has answered the request she expressed in naming her first son: Joseph means "May he add," that is, may God add another son (30:24).

Finally Jacob arrives home in Beersheba. His mother has died sometime during his absence. His father is still alive but is apparently too decrepit to play any active role. Of Isaac, we hear only of his breathing his last.

Isaac's death marks the end of an era in the family saga. Many of the characters who played a part in Jacob's earlier life have now left the stage. It is a natural point at which to look back over their lives.

Isaac emerges in the story as a man disinclined to take initiative. Unlike Abraham, Isaac did not arrange marriages for either of his sons, as would have been customary. He was outsmarted by Rebekah and Jacob—and did not rebuke them for their deception. Overall, Isaac does not display much perceptiveness. "I do not know the day of my death" (27:2), he declared, by which he meant that he thought his death was imminent. Yet Isaac lived on for more than two decades (see 35:27–28). (His words were truer than he realized!) Yet Isaac does not lack dignity. He blessed both his sons, and both prospered. In the end, it is Isaac, not Rebekah, who is honored with a funeral by his sons.

By contrast, Rebekah is a tragic figure. We may sympathize with her pursuit of her own interests. Indeed, her favoritism toward Jacob is easier to justify than Isaac's toward Esau, if we assume that she preferred to plan for a retirement with Jacob, rather than having to rely on Esau, who had shown his disrespect for her by marrying wives who treated her badly. We may admire Rebekah's ability to size up a situation and take action. Yet, while she made plans confidently, events proved her confidence to be ill-founded. "Let your curse be on me," she said to reassure Jacob (27:13). Presumably she did not think that any curse would fall on either of them; she expected Jacob to succeed. But Rebekah's incitement of Jacob to deceive Isaac had disastrous results—for her above all.

We may surmise that Rebekah's treachery alienated Esau irrevocably. The lasting damage done to her relationship with Isaac may be inferred from the narrative's silence about her death, which is not described as an occasion for her husband's profound grief and elaborate funeral arrangements—as Sarah's death was for Abraham. In fact, Rebekah's death is not even mentioned. If Rebekah incited Jacob to steal Esau's blessing in the hopes of ensuring a comfortable future for herself as a widow, she might as well have saved herself the trouble. Her husband outlived her. Rebekah's final words in the story put her overconfidence into high relief: "I will send for you," she said to Jacob (see 27:45). Events gave the lie to her confidence that she could control her destiny by deception. Jacob left, and she never saw him again.

Rachel comes across as a supportive wife, endorsing Jacob's proposal to free himself from her father's unjust management. In her own mind, we may suspect, Rachel's greatest accomplishment was leaving Jacob with two sons of her own, as well as two sons by her handmaid, Bilhah. The heritage she bequeathed to the next generation, however, was a mixed one. The spirit of competition she exhibited toward her sister, Leah, will reappear among the sons—a bitter heritage leading to the brink of fratricide.

What about the characters who remain on the stage at Isaac's death?

Most prominent, of course, is Jacob. God has been gracious to him. How well has Jacob responded? How much has he changed? Clearly, something genuine has developed in his relationship with God. After his reconciliation with Esau, he builds an altar for the first time, calling it "God Is the God of Israel"—Israel being Jacob's own new name (33:20). At Bethel he has his family purge themselves of "foreign gods" and builds another altar (35:2–7). But why has it taken so long for Jacob to move from calling God "the God of my father" (31:5) to simply "God" (33:5)?

How much has Jacob changed? At Shechem, Jacob seems curiously unmoved at his daughter's rape (34:30)—concerned about the rest of his family, but hardly cutting a heroic figure. Is this the same old Jacob, clever at calculating how to secure his blessings? As a youth, Jacob knew what it was like to be a father's not-favored son. Yet he turns around and repeats the pattern with his own sons. He goes out of his way to demonstrate that the sons of Rachel mean more to him than any of the others. This preferential treatment fuels conflict among the sons, leading to a new cycle of treachery, suffering, repentance, and reconciliation. In the course of the conflict, Jacob's sons will deceive him even more seriously than he deceived his own father (chapter 37).

Yet, on balance, God's mercy toward Jacob has not been fruitless. The older Jacob—a hardworking husband and father caring anxiously for a large family—is certainly a more creditable person than the younger Jacob, liar and thief. By God's grace, and not without some hard work and hard praying on his part, Jacob has become a man through whom God's blessing can flow down to the next generation and outward into the world (see 47:7, 10).

In some ways, Esau may come off best in this family circle. A crude young man, more interested in eating than in owning his part in God's plan for his family, he was nevertheless guileless and sincerely devoted to his father. By story's end, he has shown himself to be a magnanimous, even noble figure. Esau is profoundly moved at the sight of his brother after his long absence. He is willing to forget Jacob's sin against him.

We catch a last glimpse of Esau standing side by side with Jacob at their father's bier (see 35:29). The picture of the two brothers, reconciled through Esau's willingness to forget the past, abides as an icon of reproach to Jacob's descendants for their later hostility against the descendants of Esau—and as a reproach to all of us who engage in hatred and resentment against other nations.

We hear almost nothing more of Leah, except for Jacob's statement on his deathbed that he had buried Leah in his parent's tomb (49:31). Yet the part Leah has played has made her a crucial actor in the divinely scripted drama. Through her son Judah, she will be a foremother of the kings of Israel and ultimately of *the* king of Israel, Jesus of Nazareth. Thus, through the line of the not-preferred son, Jacob, and through the offspring of Jacob's unloved wife, Leah, the Redeemer will come into the world. Surely this is a banner case of God's pattern of working with those who seem least likely to be the instruments of his purposes. This way of going about things shows God's love for those who are otherwise unloved—and makes clear that the positive outcome is not due to human strength, cleverness, good looks, birth order, or any other attainments that we might regard as qualifications for success (compare with 1 Corinthians 1:26–31).

God, of course, has been the unseen player throughout the story. What kind of person has God shown himself to be? How are we to understand the pattern of his seeming absences, his hidden workings, and his surprising manifestations to human beings? From Jacob's experience, what might we learn about the sort of relationship that God wishes to have with each one of us? What promise does he hold out to those who respond to his kindness?

Someone's in the Field with Dinah

Tucked in between the joyful birth announcements of Leah's last son and of Rachel's firstborn is the news that Leah "bore a daughter, and named her Dinah" (30:21). Four chapters later, Dinah comes to the fore . . . sort of. Though she stands at the center of this tale of a rape and its consequences, Dinah never emerges as a person in her own right. She is as lost among the actions of others as her birth was lost among her brothers'.

Chapter 34 is so engaging and artfully constructed that you should read it if possible. But put aside any expectation of getting inside the head of a woman from an ancient culture. This story of crime and punishment advances the broader picture of the Jacob clan, hitting on themes of power and politics, human intrigue and divine protection. Along the way, it raises familiar provocative questions about the mystery of God's choosing to preserve and bless a seriously deficient father and his dysfunctional family.

Act one takes place perhaps a decade after Jacob's return to Canaan—enough time for Dinah to have grown from one of the "frail" children in Jacob's retinue (33:13) into a mobile young woman. One day she leaves the family tents, which are pitched opposite the city of Shechem, literally to "go seeing"—the Hebrew word suggests curiosity—among the local women (34:1). (These, by the way, are just the kind of people her grandparents deplored as daughters-in-law: 27:46; 28:8.) This little adventure is the only action Dinah will take. From here on out, the story presents her as the object of verbs, never the subject.

Enter Shechem, a young buck on the make. An immigrant's daughter is an easy target for this "prince of the region" whose family wields political power in the city, and he quickly has his way with Dinah. This is not consensual sex. It is a brutal rape, and the Hebrew underlines the fact with a burst of verbs: literally, Shechem "saw," "took," "laid," and "debased" his victim (34:2). But to further complicate the moral balance, three more verbs appear, signaling the fact that the rapist has fallen in love (34:3). Apparently used to getting his way, Shechem informs his father, Hamor, that he wants to take as a wife the woman he has taken by force. What Dinah wants remains a complete unknown.

Jacob is inscrutable too, showing no sign of emotion at the news of his daughter's violation. And when Hamor approaches him to negotiate the marriage, Jacob leaves the matter to his sons. One reason he keeps silent is because he feels virtually defenseless against the more powerful Canaanites (34:30). St. Ambrose regarded Jacob's approach as peace-loving restraint and pronounced it admirable. Still, it's an unnatural sort of father who acts passive and emotionally distant when his daughter is sexually assaulted.

The missing note of indignation is supplied by Jacob's sons, for whom Dinah's rape is an outrage akin to sacrilege, a thing "not to be done" (34:7). Hamor and Shechem make matters worse by offering no apology. Without so much as alluding to the crime, Hamor makes his pitch for Dinah's hand on a strictly mercenary basis, promising intermarriage, land, and business opportunities for the family. Headstrong Shechem all but dares the brothers to set an exorbitant bride price, "as high as you like" (34:9–12).

Unmoved and undoubtedly insulted by such financial inducements, the brothers stipulate just one nonnegotiable demand: that every man in the city of Shechem be circumcised. "Then we will give our daughters to you, and we will take your daughters for ourselves, and we will live among you and become one people" (34:16). The narrator has given notice that the brothers are speaking "deceitfully" (34:13)—like father, like sons. Even without this advance warning, though, some skepticism would be in order: these are people whose ancestors adamantly opposed intermarriage and cultural assimilation (24:3–4; 28:1–2).

Hamor and Shechem have no clue that forked tongues may run in Jacob's family. They accept the stipulation with alacrity and hurry home to persuade the city council that circumcision is in their best interests. But they, too, fudge the truth. Their speech deviously implies that Jacob's goods and livestock will be fair game for the Shechemites. It also edits out any allusion to young Shechem's marriage plans and courtship techniques. No alarm bells are sounded, so all the men of the city go under the knife quite willingly.

Three days later, when the Shechemites are still sore from the surgery, Simeon and Levi raid the city and put them all to the sword. While there is some poetic justice in the choice of circumcision as the punishment for rape, the mass slaughter comes as a shock. But so does the surprise revelation that Dinah has been living as a captive (34:26). Her brothers take her out of Shechem's house and bring her back home. Then, in a less edifying scene, Jacob's other sons plunder the city and take the women, children, animals, and goods as booty.

There is a fault line running through Jacob's family, and the upheaval surrounding Dinah's rape-abduction reveals it. When Jacob finally finds his voice, it is to hotly berate Simeon and Levi for their bloody deed—not for killing the innocent along with the guilty but for exposing him to reprisals. "You have brought trouble on me by making me odious to the inhabitants of the land," he rages. "If they gather themselves against me and attack me, I shall be destroyed, both I and my household" (34:30).

One gets the strong impression that Jacob might have traded Dinah for a bit of peace and quiet, even if it meant her marrying a foreigner! And where is the pious patriarch who prayed so earnestly when it looked like Esau might wipe him out (32:11–12)? Has Jacob forgotten God's interventions and promises of blessing and protection?

Simeon and Levi have the last word in this episode. Directed at Jacob, it is stinging—and loaded: "Should our sister be treated like a whore?" (34:31). They are referring, of course, to Hamor's cavalier attitude toward Dinah's virginity and his attempt to pay them off. But another possible translation targets the man who has not displayed one spark of fatherly concern: "Will he"—that is, Jacob—"treat our sister like a whore?" The implied accusation is that Jacob didn't value Dinah all that much to begin with.

There are indicators that Simeon and Levi are right on target. The story's opening words refer to Dinah as "the daughter of Leah, whom she had borne to Jacob" (34:1). The two-parent identification—rare in the Bible—is a reminder that Dinah is the child of an unloved wife. So are Simeon and Levi (29:33–34). This bond of solidarity suggests why the brothers are so zealous about doing right by their sister. Witnesses to Leah's misery, they smolder with indignation to see Dinah disrespected too. Their biting reference to her as "our sister" rather than "your daughter" sends Jacob a message. Biblical scholar Meir Sternberg observes that they "in effect wrest her out of the father's guardianship: she may not be your daughter, but she certainly is 'our sister' and no one will treat her like a whore."

Conveniently, Dinah's name derives from the Hebrew *din,* meaning "judgment" or "justice." Does she get justice? Some modern commentators think not, pointing out that her feelings are never taken into account. Viewed within the context of the culture, however, the brothers' act is clearly a vindication, a statement about Dinah's worth as an individual. At the same time, their murderous destruction of an entire city is a monstrous overreaction.

Like life itself, this story is complex and messy, with gray areas and a "happy ending" that doesn't entirely satisfy. Simeon and Levi have done right to champion Dinah, but their deceit, excess, and apparent lack of reliance on God make it difficult to approve them wholeheartedly. It is perhaps with some reluctance that the narrator leaves them the last word. The broader family story leaves it to Jacob. The deathbed "blessing" he pronounces over Simeon and Levi is no stamp of approval: "May I not be joined to their company—for in their anger they killed men. . . . Cursed be their anger, for it is fierce, and their wrath, for it is cruel!" (49:6–7).

It is significant that the first story to feature Jacob's children as characters in their own right exposes the subterranean tensions that his favoritism has caused. Though "amazing grace" is undeniably at work, it has not automatically transformed Jacob into a model husband and father. A more receptive person might have recognized his sons' rebellion as a wake-up call. Jacob does not. As a result, the destructive forces of envy and rivalry persist silently beneath the surface of ordinary family life—emotional tectonic plates whose inexorable shifting leads to another eruption—the conflict between Joseph and his brothers.

Suggestions for Bible Discussion Groups

Like a camping trip, a Bible discussion group works best if you agree on where you're going and how you intend to get there. Many groups use their first meeting to talk over such questions and reach a consensus. Here is a checklist of issues, with bits of advice from people who have experience in Bible discussions. (A planning discussion will go more smoothly if the leaders have thought through the following issues beforehand.)

Agree on your purpose. Are you getting together to gain wisdom and direction for your lives? to finally get acquainted with the Bible? to support one another in following Christ? to encourage those who are exploring—or reexploring—the Church? for other reasons?

Agree on attitudes. For example: "We're all beginners here." "We're here to help one another understand and respond to God's word." "We're not here to offer counseling or direction to one another." "We want to read Scripture prayerfully." What do *you* wish to emphasize? Make it explicit!

Agree on ground rules. Barbara J. Fleischer, in her useful book *Facilitating for Growth,* recommends that a group clearly state its approach to the following:

- *Preparation.* Do we agree to read the material and prepare answers to the questions before each meeting?
- *Attendance.* What kind of priority will we give to our meetings?
- *Self-revelation.* Are we willing to help the others in the group gradually get to know us—our weaknesses as well as our strengths, our needs as well as our gifts?
- *Listening.* Will we commit ourselves to listening to one another?
- *Confidentiality.* Will we keep everything that is shared *with* the group *in* the group?
- *Discretion.* Will we refrain from sharing about the faults and sins of people who are not in the group?
- *Encouragement and support.* Will we give as well as receive?
- *Participation.* Will we give each person the time and opportunity to make a contribution?

You could probably take a pen and draw a circle around *listening* and *confidentiality.* Those two points are especially important.

The following items could be added to Fleischer's list:

♦ *Relationship with parish.* Is our group part of the adult faith-formation program? independent but operating with the express approval of the pastor? not a parish-based group?

♦ *New members.* Will we let new members join us once we have begun the six weeks of discussions?

Agree on housekeeping.

♦ *When will we meet?*

♦ *How often will we meet?* Meeting weekly or every other week is best if you can manage it. William Riley remarks, "Meetings once a month are too distant from each other for the threads of the last session not to be lost" *(The Bible Study Group: An Owner's Manual).*

♦ *How long will meetings run?*

♦ *Where will we meet?*

♦ *Is any setup needed?* Christine Dodd writes that "the problem with meeting in a place like a church hall is that it can be very soul-destroying," given the cold, impersonal feel of many church facilities. If you have to meet in a church facility, Dodd recommends doing something to make the area homey *(Making Scripture Work).*

♦ *Who will host the meetings?* Leaders and hosts are not necessarily the same people.

♦ *Will we have refreshments?* Who will provide them?

♦ *What about child care?* Most experienced leaders of Bible discussion groups discourage bringing infants or other children to adult Bible discussions.

Agree on leadership. You need someone to facilitate—to keep the discussion on track, to see that everyone has a chance to speak, to help the group stay on schedule. Rena Duff, editor of the newsletter *Sharing God's Word Today,* recommends having two or three people take turns leading the discussions.

It's okay if the leader is not an expert on the Bible. You have this booklet, and if questions come up that no one can answer, you can delegate a participant to do a little research between meetings. It's important for the leader to set an example of listening, to draw out the quieter members (and occasionally restrain the more vocal ones), to move the group on when it gets stuck, to remind the members of their agreements, and to summarize what the group is accomplishing.

Bible discussion is an opportunity to experience the fulfillment of Jesus' promise "Where two or three are gathered in my name, I am there among them" (Matthew 18:20). Put your discussion group in Jesus' hands. Pray for the guidance of the Spirit. And have a great time exploring God's word together!

Suggestions for Individuals

You can use this booklet just as well for individual study as for group discussion. While discussing the Bible with other people can be a rich experience, there are advantages to reading on your own. For example:

♦ You can focus on the points that interest you most.
♦ You can go at your own pace.
♦ You can be completely relaxed and unashamedly honest in your answers to all the questions, since you don't have to share them with anyone!

Our suggestions for using this booklet on your own are these:

♦ Don't skip the Questions to Begin. The questions can help you as an individual reader warm up to the topic of the reading.
♦ Take your time on the Questions for Careful Reading and Questions for Application. While a group will probably not have enough time to work on all the questions, you can allow yourself the time to consider all of them if you are using the booklet by yourself.
♦ After reading the Guide to the Reading, go back and reread the Scripture text before answering the Questions for Application.
♦ Take the time to look up all the parenthetical Scripture references.
♦ Since you control the pace, give yourself plenty of opportunities to reflect on the meaning of Jacob's story for you. Let your reading be an opportunity for these words to become God's words to you.

Bibles

The following editions of the Bible contain the full set of biblical books recognized by the Catholic Church, along with a great deal of useful explanatory material:

♦ The Catholic Study Bible (Oxford University Press), which uses the text of the New American Bible
♦ The Catholic Bible: Personal Study Edition (Oxford University Press), which also uses the text of the New American Bible
♦ The New Jerusalem Bible, the regular (not the reader's) edition (Doubleday)

Books

♦ Lawrence Boadt, "Genesis," in *The International Bible Commentary: A Catholic and Ecumenical Commentary for the Twenty-First Century,* ed. William R. Farmer et al. (Collegeville, Minn.: Liturgical Press, 1998), 348–94.
♦ John S. Kselman, "Genesis," in *The HarperCollins Bible Commentary,* revised edition, ed. James L. Mays et al. (San Francisco: HarperSanFrancisco, 2000), 83–118.

How has Scripture had an impact on your life? Was this booklet helpful to you in your study of the Bible? Please send comments, suggestions, and personal experiences to Kevin Perrotta, General Editor, Trade Editorial Department, Loyola Press, 3441 N. Ashland Ave., Chicago, IL 60657.